Wicked
NEW ORLEANS

One of the women of New Orleans's Storyville. *Photograph by Ernest Bellocq.*

Wicked NEW ORLEANS

THE DARK SIDE OF THE BIG EASY

TROY TAYLOR

Charleston · London

THE
History
PRESS

Published by The History Press
Charleston, SC 29403
www.historypress.net

Unless otherwise noted, all images are from the author's collection.

First published 2010

Manufactured in the United States

ISBN 978.1.59629.945.0

Library of Congress Cataloging-in-Publication Data

Taylor, Troy.
Wicked New Orleans : the dark side of the Big Easy / Troy Taylor.
p. cm.
Includes bibliographical references.
ISBN 978-1-59629-945-0
1. Crime--Louisiana--New Orleans--History. 2. Criminals--Louisiana--New Orleans--
History. 3. Organized crime--Louisiana--New Orleans--History. I. Title.
HV6795.N38T39 2010
364.109763'35--dc22
2010018081

CONTENTS

ACKNOWLEDGEMENTS

The author would like to thank the great chroniclers of crime and legend in New Orleans, including Lyle Saxon, Herbert Asbury, Robert Tallant and Edward Dreyer, along with many other writers and chroniclers of the city's life and death. Thanks also to the jazz musicians who created an American original and to Becky LeJeune at The History Press. As always, thanks to my wife, Haven, who makes it all worthwhile.

A CITY BORN IN SIN

New Orleans is a city that was literally born in sin. From the original charters that were based on fraud to the emptying of the French prisoners to provide settlers to the region, widespread government corruption, gaudy social functions, rampant prostitution and frequent lapses in any civilized moral code, New Orleans has a long and very colorful history of crime and vice.

The corrupt city of legend and tradition began during the days of French governor Marquis de Vaudreuil and continued through the years of the city's domination by Spain. It flourished between 1800 and 1803, when the province was neither French nor Spanish, and when a general sense of freedom allowed and encouraged the arrival of vagabonds and adventurers from all parts of the world. It the end, it would be as property of the United States that New Orleans would embark upon its "golden age" of crime and spectacular wickedness and would achieve its status as America's leading city of sin.

In September 1717, John Law's Company of the West, popularly known as the Mississippi Company, obtained, by royal grant, control of the French province of Louisiana. At the time, there were almost no settlements in the region, which had long ago been claimed for France by the explorer LaSalle. The small outpost that existed nearby had a population of fewer than 300, consisting of a garrison of 124 soldiers, a few priests, 28 women and 25 children. The men were mostly adventurers and frontiersmen who had wandered into the province from Canada and Illinois, but the women, almost without exception, were deportees from the prisons and brothels of Paris. The hardships of life in the wilderness had not changed their manners and customs. When a worried priest suggested that sending away all of the immoral women would improve the culture of the province, Lamothe Cadillac, who was then governor of Louisiana, replied, "If I send away all loose females, there will be no women left here at all, and this would not suit the views of the King or the inclinations of the people."

This was not the first time that a commercial enterprise had attempted to settle Louisiana. The Bourbons of France were broke by the early 1700s. They had spent vast amounts of money on exploration and now had vast lands under their control but not the money to actually develop them. When Scotsman John Law approached them with his grand scheme, he must have seemed like a godsend. The terms of the royal franchise issued to the Mississippi Company were granted to John Law with the understanding that he would import six thousand white settlers and three thousand slaves to the colony. They would then work, as a commercial enterprise, the gold and silver mines and pearl hatcheries with which the country was said to abound. The Mississippi Company was made up of investors and a board of directors, which elected Law the chief director and gave him almost unlimited powers. Under Law's plan, France would retain all governmental control of the new colony.

Law's authority over the enterprise allowed him to place himself and his representatives in almost every position of power in the colony. However, he did appoint Jean Baptiste Le Moyne, Sieur de Bienville, as the governor and commander of the region. Bienville had been in Louisiana for twenty years and, with his brother, Iberville, had played an important role in the early exploration of the area. He knew Louisiana well, and while he accepted his appointment to the governorship, he also suspected that Law's plan was an elaborate scheme. He had repeatedly told his superiors in Paris that there were no gold and silver mines in Louisiana and that the few pearls to be found in the Gulf of Mexico were worthless. He urged the French government to abandon its search for riches and focus instead on the development of agriculture in the rich lands of the Mississippi Valley. But his recommendations were dismissed because they provided too slow of a method of garnering the boundless wealth that the French were certain Louisiana had for them. Bienville accepted his position and, while suspicious of Law, hoped that he would soon have the authority to carry out the projects that he felt would truly develop the region.

John Law was a mathematical genius and one of the most flamboyant promoters in history. His grand scheme of the New Orleans colony was doomed to fail, and eventually, the French government ended his control over it.

Bienville's commission arrived in February 1718, and soon after, he led twenty-five convicts, carpenters and a few adventurers from the Illinois country to a crescent-shaped bend in the river that he had surveyed nearly twenty years before as a good site for a settlement. In a cypress swamp that was teeming with snakes and alligators, he set his men to work clearing the forests and building sheds and barracks. He named the new settlement "Nouvelle Orleans" in honor of the French regent, the Duke of Orleans.

Work was soon underway, and Bienville sent the directors of the Mississippi Company glowing descriptions of the climate in New Orleans, the fertility of the soil and the many other advantages of the site he had chosen for the town. Other French officials, however, felt less optimistic about the site. They complained of the flat and swampy ground, the plague of crayfish, the frequent fogs, thick woods, clouds of mosquitoes and the "fever-laden" air.

There is no question that the climate has always been one of New Orleans's greatest drawbacks. All of the early visitors to the city complained of the dampness of the winter months and the heat and humidity of the summers. Shoes and other articles of clothing commonly mildewed if left overnight on the floor in some parts of the city. Cellars were unknown, and walls were often too wet for plaster to stick to them. In the early days, water was encountered from twelve to eighteen inches below the ground, and as late as the 1840s, New Orleans was known throughout America as the "Wet Grave" because of the difficulties encountered in burying corpses. An English traveler, Captain James Alexander, who visited the city in 1832 wrote,

> *Coffins are sunk to depths of three or four feet by having holes bored in them, and two black men standing on them till they fill with water, and reach the bottom of the moist tomb. Some people are particular and dislike this immersion after death; and, therefore, those who can afford it have a sort of brick oven built on the surface of the ground, at one end of which, the coffin is introduced, and the door hermetically closed, but the heat of the southern sun on this "whited sepulcher" must bake the body inside, so that there is but a choice of disagreeable after all.*

In those early days, the tradition of the aboveground tombs began, and it still continues today.

Development of the city began that year, but work was slow, thanks to brutal heat, the rising and falling waters of the Mississippi and a shortage of men and materials. While Bienville was struggling against the elements to build a city, John Law had started the next phase of his plan. With the aid and encouragement of the government, he started a land- and stock-selling campaign that soon sent all of France into a frenzy of speculation. The national currency was inflated for Law's plans, and what turned out to be a colossal fraud drove the country to the verge of financial ruin. Law had nothing to back his stock except for inflated promises of the immense profits that Louisiana was going to produce.

But to start the flow of wealth, Law needed colonists, and he was having trouble getting them. He had promised his investors that he would have a colony of six thousand settlers and three thousand slaves by 1727. To get them, the government began ransacking jails and hospitals. Disorderly soldiers, black sheep of distinguished families, political suspects, thieves, vagabonds and smugglers were kidnapped and shipped under guard to New Orleans. To those who would go willingly, the Mississippi Company promised free land, provisions and transportation to Louisiana. They were promised riches, wealth and, of course, endless variations of the gold and silver mines that did not exist.

The first colonists arrived in June 1718 and consisted of three hundred willing immigrants and nearly twice that number in soldiers and convicts. They crowded into rough sheds and tents and worked to make the best of the situation that they found themselves in. The biggest problem soon turned out to be the shortage of women. Governor Bienville begged for women to be sent to the colony because, he wrote, "The white men are running in the woods after the Indian girls." About 1720, one solution to cure the shortage of women was arrived at when the jails of Paris were emptied of prostitutes. The ladies of the evening were given a choice: serve their term in prison or become a colonist in Louisiana. Those who chose the New World quickly became the wives of the men most starved for female companionship.

The history of the region during the years of the Mississippi Company is a sad record of confusion, failure and misdirection. The investors wanted someone to blame for the suffering of the colonists who landed in such a cruel place and for the failure of the exploration parties to find any silver or gold. A radical gesture was needed to placate the horde of disappointed people who had sunk money into the scheme, so the board of directors blamed everything on Bienville. They sent a new director, Duvergier, to Louisiana and gave him authority over Bienville, although the governor was not officially dismissed. Duvergier was instructed to do whatever was necessary to get the colony back on track and, above all, to renew the search for the mythical gold, silver and pearls of the region.

Bienville didn't mind the change and now had more time to devote to the building of New Orleans. Even though Duvergier was recalled to Paris in less than a year and Bienville was restored to power, during that time Bienville was able to direct a considerable change in the physical aspect of the town. By 1727, the population had doubled, streets had been laid out and named and, in the spring of that year, Ursuline nuns had arrived in the city to start a school and hospital.

The nuns were also in charge of the *filles a la cassette*, or the "casket girls," who had been chosen from good French families to come to New Orleans and become wives of some of the upstanding local men. Before leaving France, the Mississippi Company had given each of the young women a small chest containing two coats, two shirts and undershirts, six hats and other pieces of clothing. It is believed that the nickname of these women came from the wooden chests they were given. The first "casket girls" arrived in New Orleans in 1728 and continued to arrive at regular intervals until 1751. They were all lodged together, and during the day, the men of the colony were permitted to see them in order that a choice might be made. At night, they were guarded by soldiers. Husbands were soon found for all of them.

By some strange happening, none of the prostitutes who had been brought to New Orleans as wives for the men of the colony had children. On the other

The Ursuline Convent in 1903. The building was constructed in the mid-1700s to house the Ursuline sisters and the "casket girls" who were sent over from Paris. It stands as one of the oldest surviving structures in the Mississippi River Valley. *Courtesy of the Library of Congress.*

hand, the "casket girls" seem to have been extraordinarily fertile, each becoming the mother of what must have been one hundred children who, in turn, were also blessed with large families. Proof of these biological miracles is offered by the fact that practically every native family of New Orleans is able to trace its ancestry back to one of the "casket girls" and never to those unfortunate young women who came to Louisiana instead of waiting out their sentence in jail!

But New Orleans's activities of the era did not consist of merely building a city or starting a family. In less than ten years, the city had acquired a reputation for being a town of crime and loose morals. The readymade underworld that the Mississippi Company had dumped into the region was becoming restless. Murders and robbery were becoming frequent occurrences, and it seemed that no man's life or property was safe. The rabble that had been sent to New Orleans by the Mississippi Company had been promised a life of ease, with no other labor than might be required to scoop up nuggets of gold from the ground. Work was abhorrent to many of the colonists, mostly those plucked from French prisons, and they refused to perform any actual labor. Instead, they spent their time drinking, fighting and attempting to steal enough money to enable them to leave the colony.

With no one else to do the work that needed to be done, the solution to the problem seemed to be the importation of slaves. Since most of them had been captured by slave traders in Africa, stringent laws, rigidly enforced, were necessary to keep them in line. In January 1724, Bienville began the preparation of the infamous *Code Noir* (Black Code), which was adapted from the existing laws in Santo Domingo. The law would go on to form the basis

The *Code Noir* (Black Code) was one of the first laws enacted by any southern region that actually protected slaves from mistreatment by their masters. *Courtesy of the Library of Congress.*

of the Black Code that was adopted by the Louisiana legislature after the purchase of the territory by the United States.

The code was an unusual one and unlike any other in the southern states, which protected the ownership of slaves. While it did promise severe penalties for any slave who rebelled, it also fully protected the black slave from tyranny, neglect, oppression or cruelty by his white master. Simply, slaves could not be mistreated in New Orleans, and if they were, their white owners would suffer stiff fines and perhaps even a jail sentence.

But there were other codicils to the *Code Noir*. First of all, it called for the expulsion of all Jews from the colony and prohibited any form of worship except for the Catholic faith. Masters were ordered to provide religious instruction for their slaves and promised confiscation of any slaves who were supervised by a person who was not a Catholic or was found at work on a Sunday or holy day. There were forty-nine articles that dealt entirely with the conduct and government of blacks. The code prohibited any intermingling of races, including marriage and sexual acts. It also allowed for slaves to be set free by their masters. If a free person of color lived in New Orleans, he or she was granted "the same rights, privileges, and immunities which are enjoyed by free-born persons."

Bienville signed the Black Code in March 1724 and departed for Paris. He was not involved with colonial affairs again until 1731, when the Mississippi Company surrendered its charter to the French government and the entire scheme was exposed as a fraud.

During Bienville's long absence, trouble began with the nearby Chickasaw Indian tribes. Bienville, who was respected for his diplomacy, managed to make peace with the Indians. During his time in France, the unsteady truce that he had managed to establish began to deteriorate. In 1729, Natchez Indians, allies of the Chickasaw, attacked Fort Rosalie at Natchez, slaughtering about 250 settlers and kidnapping 450 women, children and slaves. Many feared that New Orleans would be next.

The nearby Indian attacks, combined with the political disorder of the time, caused the investors in John Law's company to petition France to get rid of the unprofitable Louisiana colony. Bowing to financial pressure, France ordered the dissolution of the company's charter. The company's assets were liquidated, and the entire plan was exposed as a long recital of failure, confusion, financial mismanagement and fraud. In desperation, the French government turned to Bienville and reappointed him to his old post as governor. He returned to Louisiana in 1733 and tried to restore order, both in the city and with the restless Indian tribes. Eventually, a campaign against the Natchez and Chickasaw brought an end to these troubles.

But New Orleans was still not a pleasant place to live. There were occurrences of both flooding and drought, which caused food shortages and outbreaks of disease. In 1735, there was an epidemic of wild dogs in the city. Bienville had to send out a contingent of soldiers to hunt them down. He refused to give up on the place, though, and development continued until his retirement in May 1743.

On May 10 of that year, Bienville transferred his authority to Marquis de Vaudreuil and, soon after, departed from the colony forever. He had spent forty-five of his sixty-five years trying to carve out a civilization in the Louisiana wilderness. His weariness with the French colonial system had finally worn him down. He died in March 1767.

The Marquis de Vaudreuil was a royal governor in every sense of the word. He imitated as closely as possible the life of the French court at Versailles, throwing grand balls, elaborate state dinners and theatrical presentations that must have seemed out of place in a city with unpaved and unlighted streets, stretches of alligator-infested swamps and dingy, clapboard houses.

The Marquis de Vaudreuil brought the customs and traditions of the French court to New Orleans and became New Orleans's first truly corrupt politician. He traded positions for power, confiscated military goods and sold them and spent most of his time improving his personal fortune.

But he was determined to bring culture and color to New Orleans, and the locals appreciated him for it.

However, underneath the gaudy goings-on of Vaudreuil and his court, as many citizens and a few honest officials were aware, ran a current of corruption unequaled in New Orleans until the middle of the next century, when American politicians began to plunder the coffers of the city. The Marquis filled important government positions with relatives; he granted trade monopolies on the condition that he be given a large fee and a percentage of the profits; he confiscated and sold provisions that had been sent for the military and issued cheaper goods to the soldiers; and he spent most of his time improving his own private fortune.

The thieves, killers and prostitutes who had been sent to New Orleans by the Mississippi Company still formed, if not a majority, at least a large and disturbing minority of the region's inhabitants. Under Vaudreuil's lax rule, they thrived in the city and became more than ever the home of a vicious and criminal element who devoted themselves to stealing, fighting and drinking in the various taverns and gambling houses that had appeared along the riverfront. The area in which these resorts were situated became the first vice district in the city, making up nearly one-third of the area that became known as the French Quarter. No attempt was made to try to regulate this area until late in 1750, when it was discovered that a great deal of the paper money being circulated in the colony was counterfeit. Since the currency was issued by the Marquis, this was a blow to his private accounts, and he immediately ordered an investigation. All of the counterfeiters escaped, except for a free black named Joseph, who was tried and convicted. As punishment, he was flogged, branded on the shoulder with a fleur-de-lis and sent to the West Indies, where he was sold into slavery.

Alarmed by the conditions discovered in the investigation, the Marquis created a series of police regulations, which went into effect on February 18, 1751. This was the first attempt made by New Orleans officials to try to regulate vice, the sale of liquor and the actions of criminals in the city. Like many of the attempts that followed in the years to come, the new laws failed miserably.

Most of the taverns, brothels and gambling dens that were closed down when the laws went into effect were open and operating at full speed again when the Marquis de Vaudreuil was appointed as the governor of Canada and left New Orleans in February 1753. Not surprisingly, he celebrated his new post with an elaborate dinner for two hundred guests and a magnificent fireworks show.

He was succeeded in New Orleans by Louis Billouart de Kerlerec, an honest and well-meaning politician with the best intentions for the colony. He was appalled by the reckless spending of public money, the corruption of local officials and the villainy of the local inhabitants. He sought to correct the most obvious evils but was hampered at every turn by the corrupt politicians whom he was seeking to do away with. He was forced to deal with numerous problems during his tenure in office, not the least of which was the Seven Years' War, which was destined not only to change the map of North America but also to end French power in the New World.

The conflict, which is known as the French and Indian War in American history, began in 1755. New Orleans began to be flooded by French refugees from the north, driven out by British victories, and they found the colony to be torn by religious and political dissension. Kerlerec worked hard to placate the local Indians and to try to defend the city. Scores of farmers from the region had abandoned their homes and had come to New Orleans, where they added to the governor's troubles by clamoring for supplies and protection that the city was obliged to furnish. There was little for Kerlerec to do. No help was sent or even promised by France, which chose to abandon the American colonies and concentrate military efforts in Europe. For four years, not a single French vessel arrived at New Orleans, and there would have been a dire food shortage if the British governor of Jamaica, with more regard for his personal profit than concern for the starving colonists, had not contrived to secretly send supplies to New Orleans.

Meanwhile, the armies of England and its colonies conquered Canada and all of the French posts on the upper Ohio River. Of all of France's vast American domain, all that remained was Louisiana, which lay defenseless and at the mercy of any enemy that wanted to attack it. France had lost the war, and in 1763, the Treaty of Paris was signed. France ceded to England most of India and all of its American possessions lying east of the Mississippi River and renounced all claim to Canada and Nova Scotia. At the same time, Spain ceded to England all of its territory east and southeast of the river, including Florida, and received in return Havana, which had been captured by the British fleet. By this treaty, France retained possession of Louisiana and New Orleans, but the secret Treaty of Fontainebleau had already decided the fate of the region one year before. In that treaty, France had formally ceded to Spain "all of the country known under the name Louisiana, and also New Orleans." Nothing was known of this treaty in New Orleans until early summer of 1764, when France notified the colonists that they were now subjects of Spain. Nevertheless, Louisiana continued to be governed as a French province for several years after it became a Spanish territory.

Kerlerec was succeeded in June 1763 by Sieur d'Abadie and soon left for Paris. His successor remained in place during a time of great anxiety for the people of New Orleans. They had no idea what would become of the city under Spanish rule, and most feared that great changes were going to take place. They soon found themselves under the rule of Spanish governor Don Antonio de Ulloa, who became one of the most hated men in early New Orleans history—and the center of the first revolution to take place on the American continent.

In late 1768, six hundred New Orleanians rose up against the Spanish. The revolutionaries' ranks were most made up of Acadians, French farmers from Nova Scotia who had been driven from their homes by the Seven Years' War. They ended up in New Orleans, which they assumed was a safe haven when they arrived. They were fiercely protective of their freedom, and when they heard rumors that the Spanish planned to sell them into slavery, they revolted. On November 1, Don Antonio, terrified by the uprising, sailed for Havana.

With the expulsion of de Ulloa, the colonists believed that they had thrown off the yoke of Spain, and the conspirators discussed the formation of a republic, independent of European rule. Delegates were sent to other colonies in the region, but the plan turned out to be short-lived. His Majesty Carlos of Spain, angered by the revolution, sent a 2,600-man mercenary army to New Orleans to retake the city. Don Alexander O'Reilly, an Irishman in the service of Spain, led the force. He later earned the nickname "Bloody O'Reilly" after he sent all of the revolutionaries before the firing squad.

O'Reilly essentially placed New Orleans under martial law, ordering a census and levying taxes on the residents. He abolished the city council that existed and started his own governing body, the Cabildo, composed of judges and clerks whom O'Reilly ruled over. He got rid of all of the French laws, except for the Black Code, and put into effect all of the laws that governed other Spanish colonies in the New World. His soldiers were placed in charge of policing the city, and they carried out a reign of blood and terror.

After the terrible times with which O'Reilly inaugurated the Spanish rule in New Orleans, he and his successors actually governed the province with moderation and without the corruption that had soiled the administrations of the French governors of the past. The prosperity and general well-being of New Orleanians were far greater under the Spanish than they had ever been under the French. New business began coming to the city, mostly as American merchants who were eager to exploit the new market. Within twenty years of the onset of Spanish rule, the population of New Orleans had more than doubled. As far as commerce and the census were concerned, New Orleans had the semblance of a bustling city. However, its physical aspect was still that of a dirty, poorly built frontier settlement. Most of the houses were rough structures of cedar planks and logs, and large areas of swamp still existed within the city limits, serving as breeding places for insects and reptiles. That would all be changed, though, with the first of two devastating fires.

On March 21, 1788, a lighted candle on the altar of a chapel in the home of Don Vincente Nunez, the military treasurer to the province, set fire to draperies and soon consumed the building. Carried by a strong south wind, the flames spread quickly. As the city was constructed almost entirely of wood, the flames quickly devoured it. The fire started on Good Friday, and because of the holiday, the Capuchin monks refused to allow the church bells to ring a warning to the populace. As a result, the fire was out of control before enough men could be gathered to try to stop it. Section after section of the city was destroyed, including the government house, the jails, the residences, the business section, the church and, ironically, even the monastery of the monks who had refused the bells to be sounded. Only a row of houses along the levee was spared, along with the Ursuline Convent, which had been built from brick and tile.

The second great fire occurred on December 8, 1794. It started in a courtyard on Royal Street where some children were playing with flint and tinder. The flames spread to a nearby barn and then, fanned by a north wind, swept through a large portion of the city. More than two hundred buildings were destroyed, along with all of the stores, save for two, and several important government buildings.

The two fires turned out to be a blessing in disguise. The city that was destroyed by fire was a congested French community of poorly built wooden homes that had been badly arranged. The old part of New Orleans is still called the Vieux Carre (French Quarter) today, but all of the buildings that date from colonial times are Spanish in design and architecture. The rebuilding of the city began immediately after both disasters, and Spanish architects and builders took over the construction. The city that came from the ashes was one of brick and plaster, with heavy arches and roofs of tile. The buildings were erected flush against the sidewalks, balconies overhung the streets and shaded courtyards were placed between and behind the stately homes, hiding banana trees, fountains and flowers. The fires, and the subsequent reconstruction, were the best thing that could have happened to old New Orleans.

For those New Orleans residents still loyal to France, news came in the late 1790s that brought hope that they might once again be regarded as French citizens. News of the French Revolution reached the colony. Many of the residents became filled with patriotism, and there were cries for "liberty" in the theatres and public places. When news of the execution of Louis XVI reached New Orleans, there was open celebration. In 1800, the people of New Orleans discovered that the city had been given back to Napoleon of France as a result of the secret Treaty of San Ildefonso. But Napoleon was busy that year conquering the Turks, the Austrians and the Italians, plus ending a slave uprising on St. Domingue. Since New Orleans was struck with a terrible yellow fever epidemic, he allowed the Spanish to continue governing the colony.

By 1804, though, the city belonged to America. Napoleon needed money, and President Thomas Jefferson purchased the Louisiana Territory for the United States. The transfer of New Orleans took place on a balcony overlooking what would someday be called Jackson Square. New Orleans, along with the rest of the Louisiana Territory, was formally given to General Wilkinson and W.C.C. Claiborne, the commissioners appointed by President Jefferson. It was now officially an American city, which would not a pleasing prospect for many of the residents. American merchants, travelers and workers on the flatboats that had been bringing goods down the Mississippi River for years were not considered "civilized" by the French Creole residents of New Orleans. Many of the Americans constantly troubled the police with fighting and drinking, and American merchants were considered uncouth and their wives even more so. Although business was carried out between the two groups, there was no socializing, and even the wealthiest American merchants and their wives were snubbed by Creole society.

Because of this, the Americans created a society of their own and eventually created their own section of the city, outside of the boundaries of the Vieux Carre. Altercations between the Creole and the Americans were not infrequent, and at last, a boundary was created between the two societies. A strip of land between the French Quarter and the American section was designated as a "neutral ground" by an act of Congress in 1807. It later became known as Canal Street.

By 1810, with its mixture of French- and Spanish-speaking Creoles, Anglo-Americans, slaves and free people of color, New Orleans had become the largest city in the South and the fifth largest city in America. A new era of prosperity came to the city, and New Orleans's aristocrats filled their homes with the finest Persian rugs, crystal chandeliers and the best French wines that money could buy.

No matter how luxurious the city seemed, though, it was not a place for the weak. As in the earliest days of the colony, New Orleans remained a hot and humid place during the summer months. It was often infested with mosquitoes and was frequently plagued by cholera and other epidemics. In addition, there were the hurricanes, thunderstorms from the Gulf of Mexico and the frequent floods. The spring flooding would usually pour about two feet of muddy water and debris into the city.

To make matters worse, New Orleans was also considered to be one of America's most dangerous cities, for crime, bloodshed and murder were considered commonplace.

THE BLOODY FIELD OF HONOR

It has always been easy to find all manner of vice in New Orleans. During the first fifty years or so that New Orleans was an American city, the rough taverns and cheap brothels could usually be found in the area above Canal Street. During those days, the French Quarter offered a more elegant version of sin. There could be found the pits for cockfighting; the elegant gambling houses; the best bordellos; the finest restaurants, which were already developing a cuisine that was starting to be known around the world; and the theatres and ballrooms. And it was there that blood was often spilled over matters of honor.

Parties, social gatherings and masquerade balls were common in New Orleans during the first half of the nineteenth century. Many of the most fashionable balls were held in a plain wooden building on Conde (later Chartres) Street. It was here that young Creole men and women gathered to dance and hope to attract members of the opposite sex, always watched over by chaperons, mothers and young siblings who could watch but not take part in the festivities.

As the young women rested between dances in rows of wooden chairs, the young Creole men waited behind them in a narrow walkway, waiting for their turn on the dance floor. Most of these young men wore similar attire: long coats of bright colors and boots with fancy stitching. Each carried a sword cane, or *colchremarde*, a French sword that was wide near the hilt and tapered to a rapier-like blade. Numerous quarrels arose among the Creole men waiting for dances, and in those times, quarrels usually only had one ending—a duel.

Duels were frequently fought in New Orleans over matters of honor.

If one young man carelessly bumped into another, accidentally stepped on his toes or danced with a young lady without first learning who had appointed himself as her protector and obtaining his consent—any of these circumstances, and scores of others equally trivial, were sufficient cause for a challenge. Such challenges were issued and accepted even if the two men were normally the best of friends. Arrangements were quickly made, and the duelists and their seconds would quietly leave the ballroom and go to St. Anthony's Square, just behind the cathedral, where there was a cleared space that was concealed from the street by shrubbery. There they fought, strictly according to code, with their sword canes. Honor was satisfied in most situations with the drawing of first blood, however slight the wound, and the victor returned to the ballroom, while the vanquished duelist hurried home to bandage his cuts.

Affairs of this type were widely practiced in the city. In fact, it was said that nowhere else in North America was the Code of Honor regarded with such reverence and the duel so universally practiced as it was in New Orleans from about 1830 until just before the Civil War. This was considered the golden age of dueling in the city.

Fashionable society functions, theatre events and masquerade balls often produced duels, but their origin was not to be found only in societal slights or in differences of opinion regarding a dramatic artist. It seemed that the smallest breach of etiquette, the slightest suspicion about unfair dealing, even a bit of awkwardness was sufficient cause for a challenge, which none dared to refuse. The custom reached the limit of absurdity, with duels being fought over nothing at all. One story was recounted about six Creole youths who were walking down a nearly deserted street one night after a ball and, because the moon was just right in the sky, decided to "draw our swords and make this night memorable by a spontaneous display of bravery and skill." The evening ended with two of the young men later dying from their wounds.

In those days, quarrels among the Creoles never purposely ended in death. The unwritten laws of New Orleans society absolutely forbade it. Ironclad rules and precedents governed every detail of an altercation, and the duel, and all points of procedure, were settled with such exactness that when the adversaries finally faced one another they were "in full equality both socially and morally." In early French and Spanish times, the weapons principally used were rapier and broadsword. Later, the cumbersome pistols of the period were used, which rarely caused serious damage since they were so hard to aim.

However, when the Americans came to Louisiana, the rules of dueling began to change. They were compelled by circumstances to adopt the unknown code of the duel, and they added to it the unique idea that the whole purpose in fighting the duel was to kill one's opponent. With this in mind, they began introducing rifles and shotguns to the affairs. Some Americans had even more curious notions and, in accepting challenges from the haughty Creoles, stipulated that the duels be fought with a variety of weapons, ranging from clubs to axes. One of these strange affairs was held in 1810, in which the adversaries were armed with eight-foot sections of cypress boards. They knocked each other senseless, and the duel was declared a draw.

Accounts of New Orleans should never give the impression that such events were sanctioned by the legal authorities. The first regulations issued by Bienville for the governing of the province forbade dueling, and those laws were strengthened by every French and Spanish governor that followed. All of them issued proclamations deploring the custom and warning that the laws against it would be enforced. However, they seldom were. Even more stringent laws were enacted after Louisiana became part of the United States, but these laws were also largely ignored. In fact, not even the highest officials of the colony, and later the state, paid any attention to the laws that prohibited them from meeting on the field of honor. These men never hesitated to accept or send challenges, and many of them engaged in combat with both personal opponents and political enemies.

During the days of the French and Spanish rule, duels were often fought in St. Anthony's Square, a garden that was located directly behind St. Louis Cathedral. Sheltered from prying eyes by bushes and shrubs, sword fights continued until first blood was drawn. *Courtesy of the New Orleans Public Library.*

The Oaks that were once part of the Louis Allard plantation still stand in the City Park. Numerous duels were fought under these trees in years past.

During the French and Spanish days in New Orleans, most of the duels were fought in the cleared space in the center of St. Anthony's Square, behind the cathedral. Hidden away from prying eyes, the technically illegal affairs were often held over real and imagined slights that occurred at the ballroom on Conde Street. Later, a favorite place for duels was a place on the Metarie Road called *Les Trois Capelines* because of the three ancient Spanish moss–draped trees that grew there.

The most celebrated of dueling grounds, however, was a giant grove of trees called simply the Oaks. The spot was located on the plantation of Louis Allard, which was in those days quite some distance outside of the city. Today, it is part of the grounds of the city park. No records exist to say how many duels were actually fought beneath the spreading branches of the great oaks, but the number would likely run into the thousands, with fatalities in the hundreds. In many cases, a half dozen duels were fought in one day. On a single Sunday in 1837, ten duels were fought under the Oaks between sunrise and noon, three of which came to fatal ends. One of the occurred here was fought between Mandeville Marigny, other-in-law, Alexander Graithe, over some point of family ars, the grove of trees was the scene of a fight between ....berg of the U.S. Army and Alexander Cuvilier, who fought with broadswords on horseback. Colonel Schaumberg's horse was killed by a wild swing delivered by Cuvilier, but neither duelist was injured.

It was under the Oaks that a European scientist, Chevalier Tomasi, became engaged in a duel because he had the audacity to disparage the Mississippi River. He wrote a series of articles that not only dismissed the river as little more than a small stream but also made unkind references about the women of New Orleans and the superiority of Europeans over Americans. The Creoles in the city found him very offensive, and one night, anger boiled over when the chevalier was spouting his views in a coffee shop. An enraged Creole challenged him on the field of honor. They met under the Oaks at dawn, and the Creole upheld the honor of New Orleans, the local ladies and the Mississippi River by slashing the scientist across the mouth. Tomasi surrendered, but not without the last word. He would have won the duel, he claimed, if not for the inferiority of his American sword.

One of the most famous duelists of old New Orleans was Bernard Marigny, a member of one of Louisiana's oldest and most influential families. He was a master swordsman and a crack shot with a pistol and had engaged in a number of duels from which he emerged the victor. He was elected to the state legislature in 1817, and as a member of the House of Representatives, he was actively involved in many of the disputes that arose between the Creoles and the Americans in the early 1800s.

During this period, Catahoula Parish was represented in the legislature by James Humble, a blacksmith and former resident of Georgia, who was noted for his great stature, standing almost seven feet tall in his bare feet. On one occasion, Humble heard one of Marigny's speeches and made some comments that were so pointed that the Creole was grievously insulted. He challenged Humble to a duel. The Georgian was perplexed by the custom and told a friend that he refused to fight the man over an offhanded remark. Gentleman fought duels, he understood, but he was no gentleman, he was a blacksmith.

Humble was assured, however, that he would be ruined both politically and socially if he refused the challenge. His friend pointed out to him that, as the challenged party, he would have the choice of weapons and could choose something that would put him on more equal terms with his skilled adversary. Humble considered the matter for a day or two and then sent a reply to Marigny: "I accept your challenge, and in the exercise of my privilege I stipulate that the duel shall take place in Lake Ponchartrain in six feet of water, sledge hammers to be used as weapons."

Since Marigny was barely over five and a half feet tall and so slight that he could barely lift a sledgehammer, Humble certainly had the greatest advantage. Marigny's friends urged him to stand on a box and take the chance of having his skull crushed in order to retain his honor, but instead he declared that it was impossible to fight a man with such a great sense of humor. The two men worked out their differences and became close friends.

Before the Civil War, there was hardly a man in public life in New Orleans who had not fought at least one duel. Most of them had engaged in several. The first American governor of Louisiana, W.C.C. Claiborne, left the gubernatorial chair to fight Daniel Clark, a member of Congress who had been American consul in New Orleans during the final years of the Spanish regime. Clariborne's brother-in-law and secretary, Micajah Lewis, was killed in a duel with a man who had been called to account for an attack on the governor's policies. Emile La Sere, a representative in Congress from New Orleans, fought eighteen duels in the course of his political career. George A. Waggaman, a U.S. senator from Louisiana, was killed in 1843 by Dennis Prieur, who had been mayor of New Orleans from 1828 to 1838, in a duel that came about because of a violent political contest waged that year between Whigs and Democrats.

Another famous duel that came out of that campaign was fought the same year by John Hueston, editor of the *Baton Rouge Gazette*, and Alcee La Branche, a Democratic candidate for Congress from the Second District in New Orleans. During the political campaign, the *Gazette* published an article that encouraged the people of the Second District not to vote for a man who was destitute of spirit and manhood. La Branche, although he had never fought a duel before, felt that Hueston had insulted him, his party, his friends, his family and the voters of New Orleans. When Hueston visited the city a short time later, La Branche confronted him in the billiard room of the St. Charles Hotel and demanded an apology. Hueston refused, and La Branche knocked him to the floor with a billiard cue, beating him so badly that the newspaper editor was forced to remain in bed for several days. While he was recuperating, arrangements were made for a duel by friends of the two men. The chosen weapons were double-barreled shotguns. A distance between the two men was agreed upon to be forty yards.

A large crowd gathered at dawn, and the duel commenced. Both men discharged their weapons at the same time. Hueston's shot went wide of the mark, but one of La Branche's slugs passed through the editor's hair and his coat. A second exchange of shots also produced no injuries. Hueston's second, Richard Hagan, suggested that the distance between the two men be shortened or the duel called off. General John L. Lewis, La Branche's second, suggested that the duel be brought to an end also, but Hueston refused. He was determined, he said, to either kill or be killed. Preparations were then made for a third exchange of shots, in which Hueston received a small scalp wound. His own seconds then suggested that since he had been hurt—and first blood drawn—he should retire from the field. Hueston again refused, and the guns were loaded for a fourth exchange.

When the word was given, Hueston immediately fired both barrels of his gun without effect. La Branche fired one of his barrels, and the editor dropped his gun and stumbled forward. La Branche fired again before he realized that his opponent had been hit, and Hueston collapsed, shot through both lungs. He was taken to a hospital, where he died after a few hours of terrible agony.

A few weeks after this encounter, a rifle duel took place that also earned a legendary place in the history of New Orleans's affairs of honor. The participants in this affair were an English cotton merchant named Wright and Colonel S.L. Oakey, a wholesale and commission merchant who had moved to the city from New York in the 1830s. Colonel Oakey, who was well liked in the city, began having difficulties with Wright after a series of letters appeared in the *Vicksburg Sentinel* accusing the cotton merchants of New Orleans of unfair business practices. Colonel Oakey assumed the championship of the New Orleans merchants and, having tracked down Wright as the source of the letters, challenged the Englishman to a duel. Wright, who often boasted of his skills with a rifle, chose it as the weapon. Colonel Oakey, though, had never held a rifle in his hands, let alone fired one. To make matters worse, he refused to practice. When the duelists faced each other at a distance of sixty yards, Colonel Oakey's second handed him a rifle and showed him how to work the action. When the word was given, Wright fired quickly and wildly, while Colonel Oakey calmly raised his rifle and shot the Englishman through the heart.

After the Civil War, when most of the young duelists returned from the Confederate military, they found that affairs of honor were no longer in fashion. Many things had changed in the city, and there was no place for duels amid the problems and difficulties of the Reconstruction period.

UNDER THE BLACK FLAG

THE PIRATE JEAN LAFITTE

W hat most modern readers think of as piracy, practiced by such infamous characters as Blackbeard, came to an end in the Gulf of Mexico around the middle of the eighteenth century. The western seas had been swept clean of bloodthirsty buccaneers by the combined might of England, France and Spain. However, the commerce of the Gulf continued to be plundered, under the flimsy guise of legality, by privateers. These were armed ships whose captains carried letters issued by nations at war, giving them the authority to capture vessels that flew the enemy flag. Under maritime law, a privateer could keep both a captured ship and its cargo, provided he brought the prize into a port of the country to which he claimed allegiance and presented it to an admiralty court. He could then sell the loot however he pleased.

In the early 1800s, the Gulf of Mexico swarmed with pirate ships, most of which operated safely within international law by flying the flag of the Republic of Cartagena. This is now one of the principal seaports of Columbia, but in those days, it had revolted against the rule of Spain. The privateers who flew the republic's flag were supposed to prey only on Spanish ships, but most attacked every ship they came upon, regardless of nationality. With the crew of the captured ship murdered, its stores looted and the ship itself scuttled—dead men told no tales.

After America took over New Orleans and the Mississippi River became a free waterway, the western territories were open to trade. This made the city a principal market for pirates and privateers. Instead of making the

Pirates and privateers sailed the Gulf of Mexico for many years before Jean Lafitte, but he was the first to turn their plundering in an organized crime. *Courtesy of Harry Cimino.*

long voyage to Cartagena for an admiralty hearing, they could bring their prizes directly to New Orleans. In order to do this, the illegal cargoes had to be smuggled to shore since only goods that were legally noted as spoils of war could be cleared through U.S. customs. Smuggling was dangerous and required quite a bit of planning and organization, so the privateers realized the need for a base that was close to New Orleans and yet inaccessible enough that it would be safe from prying warships. They found such a place about sixty miles south of the city in the Bay of Barataria, a largely unknown spot that was separated from the Gulf by the islands Grand Terre and Grand Isle. A passage that was deep enough for seagoing vessels flowed between the islands, provided that pilots knew the channel. At the northern end of the bay, a dozen bayous led into the swamps. From this tangle of water and cypress, smugglers had been operating since the earliest days of French rule, and it had long been used as a hideout for any pirates who wanted to disappear from sight.

On Grand Terre, hidden in the trees that shielded their activities from the Gulf, the privateers established a headquarters and soon began supplying the merchants of New Orleans with contraband goods of every kind. The makeshift settlement became a rendezvous point for not only privateers, pirates and smugglers but also criminals and adventurers of every kind. Fights, robberies and fatal clashes over the division of spoils became commonplace, and it wasn't long before the New Orleans merchants began to fear visiting

Although no known photographs or accurate portraits of Jean Lafitte remain in existence, this is perhaps the most popular image of the pirate. *Pictorial History of Texas, 1879.*

the island and having any sort of dealings with the privateers. Business at Grand Terre was shabbily conducted, with every man for himself, and it soon became clear that a leader was needed to take matters into hand and bring order out of the chaos.

The man who stepped into that role was Jean Lafitte. Little is known about Lafitte's past. According to numerous sources, he appears to have been born in a dozen different places in France and to have died in as many places in the West Indies. Most likely, he was born in Bordeaux, France, in 1780 and first established himself with his brother, Pierre, in New Orleans about 1806. They established a blacksmith shop on St. Phillip Street and a store on Royal Street. Using both of these places as a front, they operated for two years as smuggler's agents.

During this time, the brothers prospered and entertained lavishly at their mansion at Bourbon and St. Phillip Streets. Jean Lafitte became well known among the businessmen and merchants and was always able to find company with the lovely young women of the city. He was a man of great personal charm and spoke several languages—English, French, Spanish and Italian—fluently. Although his profits were great and life in New Orleans was pleasant, Lafitte became dissatisfied with the way the smugglers and privateers conducted their affairs. He saw the need for a guiding hand in their business—which, in turn, would bring even greater profits to the brothers Lafitte.

Lafitte's unhappiness with the situation increased on January 1, 1808, when a new element was added to the smugglers' operations. On that date, a law went into effect that banned the further importation of slaves into the United States. Throughout the South, the price of slaves rose immediately, and plantation owners were soon glad to pay from $800 to $1,000 for an able-bodied man who could be bought for $20 on the African coast or for $300 in Cuba, which was not the headquarters of the legal slave trade. Slaves had suddenly become very important pieces of merchandise, and smuggling them into Louisiana had become immensely profitable.

Lafitte's decision about what to do with the smugglers was made for him when he learned that actual warfare threatened between the smugglers and a group of privateers who had seized a cargo of slaves that had been imported by the smuggling operation and were selling them for one dollar per pound. The privateers had managed to seize the ship when it was on its way to Grand Terre. Laffite left his business in New Orleans in the hands of his brother and went out to Barataria Bay, a two-day journey by boat through the swamps. He would face stiff opposition from some of the cutthroats on the island, including renowned pirate Rene Beluche, a man known as *Nez Coupe* or "Cut Nose" because of a slash across his face, and Vincent Gambi, a short-tempered Italian who was feared for the number of men he had killed. Lafitte also met Dominique You, who had been an artilleryman in Napoleon's army and later became one of Lafitte's principal lieutenants. These men were the most important leaders at Grand Terre, but there were others of equal prominence, and with their followers, the ruffians added up to between four and five hundred outlaws. In addition, there were almost two hundred women on the island, all of questionable character.

Lafitte faced these men alone. He met with them, carefully cataloging their faults and mistakes, and pointed out how they could achieve greater prosperity if they were organized. His arguments were so persuasive and his demeanor so convincing that, within a week, they had agreed to his terms and appointed him the leader of the newly organized band.

Lafitte ruled Grand Terre and Barataria Bay for almost a decade, and only once was his captaincy questioned. At one of his early conferences with the privateer captains, he warned all of them that Barataria Bay ships must have letters from a country at war with Spain and that only Spanish vessels could be attacked. Vincent Gambi was unhappy with this and stormed out of the conference. He began trying to get his men, as well as the other captains, to revolt against Lafitte's leadership. A short time later, one of Gambi's lieutenants came to the place where Lafitte was staying and called for him to come out. When Lafitte stepped into the doorway, the man cried that he would only take orders from Gambi. Without a word, Lafitte drew a pistol and shot the man dead. The gesture was quickly understood by everyone on Grand Terre, and no further talk of rebellion was heard.

Whether he was a pirate, smuggler or thief, Jean Lafitte was a genius at organization. Within an amazingly short time, he had united the warring factions of Grand Terre and made their business a sound one. They sailed where and when he directed, coolly walked away with stolen plunder and placed it into his hands for disposal. More and more Gulf pirates joined up with Lafitte, and a year after coming to Grand Terre, he had one thousand men at his disposal. Fifty of his ships, all flying the flag of Cartagena, swept the shipping lanes of the Gulf and came directly to Barataria Bay with their prizes. Meanwhile, Lafitte improved the conditions at Grand Terre, building thatched cottages for the pirates and their women and establishing gambling houses, cafes and brothels. Enormous warehouses for the stolen plunder were erected, along with slave quarters, where captives in chains waited to be purchased. In the center of the colony, Lafitte built himself a mansion of brick and stone, filled with the finest furniture, linens and carpets—all stolen by his band of pirates. There he entertained merchants and businessmen from New Orleans, plantation owners and slave traders, all of whom were delighted by the luxury amid which he lived.

Lafitte's business was so efficient that by 1813, practically all of the stores in New Orleans were being stocked with his smuggled merchandise, and the legitimate commerce of the city began to suffer. It was clear that within a few years, Lafitte would have a monopoly on most of Louisiana's trade. Government officials made a few halfhearted attempts to damage the Barataria Bay operations with a few inconsequential seizures, but this only served to increase Lafitte's prestige. When Governor W.C.C. Claiborne issued a proclamation in early 1813 denouncing the Barataria Bay men as pirates and warning the people of New Orleans to have no further dealings with them, Lafitte made a point of returning to the city. He and Pierre began a season of entertainment, securing the attendance of the most prominent merchants at their dinners and parties. They appeared in local restaurants, surrounded by influential friends, and boldly announced in the newspapers the dates of upcoming sales of merchandise and slaves. A few months later, Governor Claiborne issued another proclamation, which was posted in prominent places in New Orleans, offering a reward of $500 for the arrest and delivery of Jean Lafitte to the sheriff of Orleans Parish. Lafitte responded by issuing a proclamation of his own, also posted in prominent locations in the city, that offered a $1,500 reward for the arrest of Governor Claiborne and his delivery to Grand Terre.

Outraged, Claiborne filed charges against Lafitte and convinced a grand jury to return indictments against him and the other men of Barataria Bay, charging them with piracy. Pierre Lafitte, indicted with aiding and abetting his brother, was arrested and jailed. Jean immediately retained two of New Orleans's most distinguished attorneys, John R. Grymes and Edward Livingston, and offered them $20,000 each to defend his brother. Grymes was the district attorney of Orleans Parish at the time, and he resigned from office in order to collect the fee. When his successor stated in open court that Grymes had been "seduced by the bloodstained gold of pirates," Grymes challenged him to a duel. During the altercation, Grymes shot him through the hip, and the man was crippled for life.

Unfortunately, the combined skills of the two attorneys failed to get the indictment against Pierre dismissed, and he languished in jail for several months. He was eventually freed during a mysterious jailbreak. Nevertheless, Jean Lafitte agreed to pay the attorneys the large fee that he had promised.

He invited them to Grand Terre so that he could pay them in person, and while Grymes readily accepted, Livingston declined, authorizing Grymes to collect his portion of the fee at a commission of 10 percent. Grymes received his money on the day that he arrived at the pirate stronghold, but he lingered on the island, seduced by Lafitte's hospitality—and by the gambling and women that were offered him. By the end of three days, he had gambled away all of the money that he had earned, as well as the 10 percent commission that he had been given by Livingston.

Lafitte may have been at the height of his power during this period, but his popularity was beginning to wane. Even those merchants who availed themselves of the merchandise that he offered began to fear that his monopoly on trade in the region would eventually hurt them. In addition, the national government, worrying over the successes of the British during the War of 1812, at last listened to Governor Claiborne and sent a strong force against the pirates at Barataria Bay. This expedition, consisting of six gunboats and several small but heavily armed vessels, sailed from New Orleans in September 1814. The pirates were taken by surprise, and after a brief battle, the settlement at Grand Terre was destroyed and the U.S. Navy captured nine ships and nearly one hundred prisoners. Jean and Pierre Lafitte, along with several hundred of the other men, escaped into the bayous.

As far as Lafitte's personal fortunes went, fate again turned in his favor. A few days before the U.S. Navy attacked Grand Terre, an English ship appeared in Barataria Bay. After a long conversation with Lafitte, the British commander offered the pirate $30,000 in gold and a captaincy in the British navy if he would enlist his men on the side of the English during an attack on New Orleans. Lafitte asked for time to consider the offer and learned what he could of the British plans. After they sailed, Lafitte sent a full account of what had occurred to Governor Claiborne. He offered to join with the American navy and aid in repelling the invasion. In return, he asked for a pardon or "an act of oblivion for all that has been done hitherto." Claiborne called a meeting with military officials. Putting aside his previous feelings about the pirate, he told them that he believed Lafitte's story was true, and he urged them to accept the offer and recall the expedition against Barataria Bay. But the military refused to go along with it, and the attack continued as originally ordered.

Lafitte escaped the attack and fled to New Orleans where, surprisingly, he renewed his offer to the governor. Claiborne once again went to General Andrew Jackson, who had already rejected the offer and referred to the Barataria Bay men as "hellish banditti." However, as it now appeared that

General Andrew
Jackson.

an invasion was truly imminent, and Jackson knew how weak the city's
defenses actually were, he accepted. Lafitte's captured pirates were released
from jail, and the brothers Lafitte were mustered into the American military.

On December 23, 1814, the American forces, led by Andrew Jackson,
attacked British troops that made good on their plans to invade New
Orleans. The British forces were led by General Pakenham, and although
fresh from defeating Napoleon, they suffered a severe blow at the hands of

The assistance that Lafitte's pirates and smugglers gave to the army during the Battle of New Orleans earned Lafitte and his men a pardon from the president for all of their past crimes. Within a short time, they were back to committing new ones. *Courtesy of the Library of Congress.*

ragtag troops made up of Kentuckian Long Rifles, ill-prepared militiamen, Indians, Creoles, free men of color and Lafitte's pirates. The fighting raged back and forth for several bitterly cold days between Christmas and New Year's Day. The British continued to be reinforced with fresh troops until they greatly outnumbered the American forces in New Orleans.

On New Year's Day, the British attacked the city's hastily erected defenses but were driven back. One week later, the final battle took place, and once again, the battle-hardened British were no match for the gallant men of New Orleans. The militia troops and the pirates savaged the British lines without mercy. The invaders were beaten and withdrew from American shores. Ironically, soon after the battle, news finally reached the city that the British had signed a peace treaty at Ghent on Christmas Eve—two weeks before the Battle of New Orleans. The war had ended long before the final battle had even been fought.

Jackson, although originally skeptical of the role Lafitte and his men would play in the defense of New Orleans, spoke well of them in a dispatch that he wrote to the War Department on January 21, 1815:

Captains Dominique and Beluche, lately commanding privateers at Barataria, with part of their former crews and many brave citizens of New Orleans, were stationed at Batteries Three and Four. The general cannot avoid giving his warm approbation of the manner in which these gentlemen have uniformly conducted themselves while under his command, and of the gallantry with which they redeemed the pledge they gave at the opening of the campaign to defend the country. The brothers Lafitte have exhibited the same courage and fidelity, and the general promises that the government shall be duly apprised of their conduct.

The smoke from the cannons had scarcely cleared before Lafitte's lawyers, Grymes and Livingston, filed suit to recover the vessels that the military had captured at Grand Terre before the battle. At the same time, the attorney general of the state, John Dick, suggested to Governor Claiborne that the dismissing of all charges against the men of Barataria Bay would be a fitting and popular gesture. Claiborne agreed, and he, along with General Jackson, had sent letters to President Madison to notify him of the brave conduct of the pirates during the fighting. On February 6, 1815, the president signed a free and full pardon of any of the pirates who could produce a statement from Governor Claiborne that he had taken part in the battle. The brothers Lafitte, along with scores of smugglers and pirates, soon became free citizens of the United States.

There are many reasons to believe that after the battle, Jean Lafitte intended to set himself up as a gentleman in New Orleans and conduct legitimate business. Even before he was pardoned, though, an incident occurred that had much to do with determining his future.

At the great Victory Ball that was given on January 23, 1815, celebrating the defeat of the British, Lafitte approached a group that included Governor Claiborne, Andrew Jackson and Generals Coffee and de Flaugeac. Jackson and Claiborne greeted him warmly, but as Lafitte walked up to the group, de Flaugeac turned his back to him to speak to a friend. To make matters worse, when Claiborne introduced him to General Coffee, the other man hesitated before extending his hand. At that, with a devilish gleam in his eye, Lafitte introduced himself to the military man—"Lafitte, the pirate," he sneered.

Although both General Coffee and General de Flaugeac apologized and assured Lafitte that they meant no insult, the incident was said to have given Lafitte a taste of the reception that he would now receive in New Orleans business and society. He would always be "Lafitte the pirate."

Soon after the ball, he made plans to leave New Orleans. The ships that had been captured at Grand Terre before the battle were offered at government auction and purchased by one of Lafitte's financial backers. A few weeks later, he received his pardon from President Madison and sailed away to embark on a career as a privateer. With him went one hundred of the Barataria Bay men, for whom life in the city had already soured.

Jean and Pierre Lafitte attempted to establish a new base of operations at Port-au-Prince, but the governor of the city compelled them to leave after supplying them with food and water. For the next three years, the brothers roamed the Gulf of Mexico, searching for a new home and occasionally seizing a Spanish ship and smuggling the plunder into New Orleans. Eventually, in 1816, they founded a small colony off the coast of Texas that came to be known as Galvez-Town (later Galveston). There Lafitte prospered for several years, building himself a grand home and attracting several hundred men much like the ones he commanded at Grand Terre. Lafitte attempted to gain respect and protection from the governments of Mexico, Texas and even Washington, D.C., but his schemes never succeeded. Galvez-Town never managed to develop into the orderly community that he had founded on Grand Terre. It became a refuge not only for pirates and privateers but for criminals and fugitives as well from all over the region. Instead of preying on vessels that were specified in the letters from Cartagena, they resorted to outright piracy and attacked any vessel they found, regardless of what flag it was flying.

Early in September 1819, Lafitte purchased a schooner in New Orleans that he dubbed *Bravo*. He instructed two of his lieutenants, Jean Desfargues and Robert Johnson, with a crew of sixteen men, to sail the vessel to Galvez-Town. Although the ship carried no privateer's commission, it attacked a Spanish merchant vessel in the Gulf. Desfargues, Johnson and the other men were still looting the ship when the American revenue cutter *Alabama* appeared and captured them after a short fight. The ship and the pirates were taken back to New Orleans. All of the men were tried, found guilty and sentenced to hang.

Lafitte tried to find legal aid for his men. Then, joined by old friends and many planters who feared the loss of profitable business in slaves and other contraband, he caused such a stir that the authorities ordered out the militia to prevent a possible attack on the prison. In the end, though, all of the legal maneuvering and threats of violence accomplished nothing. Reprieves were granted to all of the condemned men, and one, John Tucker, was pardoned by President Monroe. When the reprieves expired, however, the remaining seventeen men were hanged as pirates.

The beginning of the end of Lafitte's headquarters in Galvez-Town came in late 1820, when a pirate named Brown plundered an American vessel in Matagorda Bay. Brown's trail led straight back to Lafitte's colony. Although Lafitte tried Brown and hanged him on an island in the harbor, the government decided that Galvez-Town had to be destroyed. Early in 1821, an American warship anchored off the coast, and Lafitte was given three months to abandon his settlement. It returned in May and found Lafitte supervising the destruction of the colony. The settlement was burned, and Lafitte sailed away in three ships, two of which abandoned him a few days later when he refused to attack a convoy of Spanish merchant ships.

What became of Lafitte after that is officially unknown. Most historians believe that the man who was once known as the "terror of the Gulf" became little more than a petty pirate and thief. He sailed from a squalid base on the coast of the Yucatan and allegedly died of fever in the town of Teljas in 1826.

It was a quiet and sad end to the life of a man who made such a mark on the history of New Orleans.

"ROLL THE BONES"

GAMBLING IN NEW ORLEANS

Modern historians have never been able to discover how gambling actually began, but it's been a part of every civilization since the beginning of recorded history. In those days, games of chance were carried out with a makeshift version of what we think of as dice—marked animal bones. The modern version of "rolling the bones" continues today.

There was undoubtedly gambling going on in New Orleans within days of the city's founding. However, the glamour of the gambler arrived with the first steamboats on the Mississippi Rivers. In the early days of steamboat navigation, the gambler was tolerated only so long as no one complained. There were many occasions, though, when he was forced to surrender his winnings and was thrown off the vessel without ceremony. Socially, he was an outcast, and in that respect, his status was unchanged even by death. A gambler was among eleven people scalded to death when an engine exploded near Bayou Sara in the early 1800s. The captain noted in his journal that the gambler "was buried separately."

In later years, though, gambling on the river was recognized as an established institution. Many steamboat captains considered it bad luck to leave the wharf without a professional gambler on board, and no attempt was made to bother him when he set up operations in the bar or the main saloon. He was in his heyday from about 1835 to the Civil War, when between six hundred and eight hundred gambling men regularly worked the big boats between St. Louis and New Orleans. During this period, the era of the "floating palaces," gamblers were an accepted part of riverboat

While gambling had been in New Orleans since the founding of the colony, the golden age of gambling began with the arrival of the steamboats—often called "floating palaces"—on the Mississippi River. *Courtesy of the Library of Congress.*

travel. They were known for their smooth demeanor, cultured manner and fancy dress.

Jimmy Fitzgerald, a New Orleans man who made—and lost—a fortune playing poker and faro on the river in the 1840s, was considered the best-dressed gambler of his time. He wore imported boots from Paris, had four overcoats and scores of expensive suits and wore a gold chain that was said to be as big around as a man's finger. He was a reckless and spectacular player, and what he won on the river he usually lost in the gambling houses on shore.

If there was anyone who competed with Fitzgerald as a fancy dresser, it was probably Jim McLane, whose family paid him $10,000 a year to stay away from home. Tom Mackey, who also sent away to Paris for his boots, was another sharp dresser. There was also Starr Davis, for whom a champion racehorse was named and who eventually became a heavy drinker and was killed after a fall down a flight of stairs. And Napoleon Bonaparte White, better known as Poley, who came to New Orleans from Washington as a boy and became a gambler after first working as a steamship engineer. After the Civil War, he married and settled in New Orleans, where he operated a gambling house on St. Charles Avenue. The house prospered, but most of his winnings were spent trying to keep his two sons, Benny and Jimmy, out of trouble. Both of the boys came to bad ends. Benny died of alcoholism in jail while awaiting trial for a shooting, and Jimmy was last heard from in California, where he killed two men over a bottle of wine. In 1889, broke and upset over a new anti-gambling ordinance that the police planned to enforce, Poley borrowed a few dollars from a Royal Street bartender and bought a revolver and an ounce of sulphate of morphine. He called on all of his friends, wished them goodbye and then went home and killed himself.

Another fashionable gambler of the era was Colonel Charles Starr, a tall, handsome man who was not only one of the most famous gamblers of the decade before the Civil War but was also regarded as the biggest liar on the river. He claimed to own dozens of plantations between New Orleans and St. Louis and only gambled because he was so bored with his uncountable wealth. Character flaw aside, he had a great wit and a dashing air that attracted men as his friends and women as his lovers. More stories were probably told about him than any other gambler on the Mississippi. He accumulated a sizable fortune during his gambling days, but in his later years, he lost his money in futile attempts to break the faro banks in New Orleans and St. Louis. When he finally ran out of money, he was driven to cadging food and drink wherever he could. One night he walked into a New Orleans restaurant where he had been a frequent and welcome guest during his days of prosperity and ordered an elaborate dinner. The manager demanded payment in advance, and without a word, Colonel Starr left the place. He returned an hour later with five dollars, which he had obtained by pawning his overcoat, and ordered the best dinner that he could for that amount. When it was served, he carefully and deliberately turned his plate upside down and dumped the food onto the table. Then he walked out once more, never looking back. He died later that same night.

The majority of gamblers on the Mississippi were known, in the vernacular of the river traveler, as "sure-thing players," which was a nice way of saying that they were crooked and would cheat any man out of his money. They were adept at palming cards and dealing from the bottom of the deck. They often used cheating devices like vest and sleeve hiding spots, mirrors for reading the cards of their opponents and poker rings fitted with small needles for making tiny indentions in the cards. Most of the big scores on the riverboats were made with marked decks, which were planted ahead of time with bribed bartenders who would send them over to the table when a fresh deck was called for.

But not every gambler was a cheat. There were many men who were known as "square players" who depended entirely on their luck and skill. Among the most celebrated were Dick Hargraves, John Powell and Major George M. White, who worked as a professional gambler for sixty-two years. Hargraves, a slim, dapper man, came to New Orleans from England about 1840. He first worked as a bartender but turned to gambling after winning $30,000 in a poker game with a sugar planter named Dupuy. Hargraves gambled on the river for more than a decade with great success. At the height of his renown, he became involved in an affair with the wife of a New Orleans banker and killed the banker when the man challenged him to a duel. Then the brother of the wife sent word that he planned to kill Hargraves if he laid eyes on him. The two men met in a seedy bar in Natchez, and Hargraves killed him, too. When he returned to New Orleans, his lover stabbed him and committed suicide. While he seemed unlucky at this point, Hargraves recovered, married and became a major in the Union army at the start of the Civil War. He died in Denver of tuberculosis in the late 1880s.

John Powell, a native Missourian, lived in New Orleans whenever he was ashore. He was the epitome of the riverboat gambler—tall, handsome, distinguished, well dressed and possessing charm and a personality that made him welcome in the best of society anywhere on the Mississippi. During his years of greatest success—from about 1854 to 1858—he was considered the most skilled poker player on the river and often backed everything he possessed on a single hand of cards. He was probably the most consistent winner of all of the "square" gamblers who worked the riverboats. At the height of his success, he owned a theatre and other property in New Orleans, a farm stocked with horses and slaves in Tennessee and considerable real estate in St. Louis. His friends often urged him to retire with his fortune, but Powell insisted that gambling was in his blood.

His career ended in 1858. That summer, he took part in a famous poker game aboard the steamship *Atlantic* with two other professional gamblers and Jules Devereaux, a wealthy Louisiana planter. Within an hour after play had begun, there was more than $37,000 on the table. The game continued without intermission for three days, during which the four men, drinking only the finest wines, ran up a bar bill of $791.50. Devereaux lost almost $100,000, and Powell took at least half of it from him. It was to be the renowned gambler's final triumph.

A few months after this memorable game, Powell played poker with a young English tourist and managed to win $8,000 and all of the man's luggage. The next morning, after breakfast, the Englishman came on deck,

Poker was not the only game of chance played on board the riverboats, but it was one of the most popular and was the reason that many fortunes came and went. *Courtesy of the Library of Congress.*

shook hands with the other passengers and then put a pistol to his head and shot himself. Powell sent the young man's money and belongings to his relatives in England and didn't gamble again for more than a year. When he returned to the river, both his luck and skill had deserted him. He never won another pot after his tragic win over the Englishman. Within a year, he had lost all of his money and his property and become a ruined, desperate man. He went to Seattle after the start of the Civil War and died in poverty in 1870.

Poker was not the only game played on the riverboats. Just about every game of chance known to man appeared on the boats at one time or another. Poker was the most popular, but it was played alongside faro, blackjack, three-card monte and the shell game.

Faro, one of the oldest of all card games, was known on the river as "the tiger." Playing it was called "bucking the tiger," and it was popular due to its fast action, easy-to-learn rules and better odds at winning than most games of chance. The game has always held a strange allure for professional gamblers. Most of them usually lost at faro, when ashore, all of the money they had won at their own specialty aboard the riverboat.

In their essentials, three-card monte and the shell game were very similar, since both took advantage of the fact that the hand is quicker than the eye, although effective manipulation of the shells required greater dexterity. The monte operator simply displayed three cards, usually two aces and a queen, and threw them down on a flat surface and bet the mark that he couldn't find the queen. The shell man moved a dried pea or a little rubber ball rapidly back and forth under three cups made of wood or metal. The sucker, having staked his money, was invited to lift the shell under which the item was hidden. If the gambler knew his business, it wasn't under any of them—it was between two of his fingers. Both types of gamers were usually assisted by "cappers" who got the game started, posing as a prospective player, and showed the suckers how easy the game was to win.

The most successful of the monte operators were William Jones, better known as Canada Bill, and George Devol, who learned to cheat at cards at age eleven. Jones and Devol worked the steamboats together for many prosperous years, although both men usually managed to lose their winnings playing faro when they went ashore.

Canada Bill stood out among the other gamblers of the era because of his slovenly appearance. Probably no man on the Mississippi looked less like a riverboat gambler. He was described as "a medium-sized, chicken-headed, tow-haired sort of man with mild blue eyes and a mouth nearly ear to ear, who walked with a shuffling, half apologetic sort of gait, and who, when his countenance was in repose, resembled an idiot. His clothes were always several sizes too large. He had a squeaking, boyish voice, and awkward, gawky manners, and a way of asking fool questions and putting on a good-natured grin, that led everybody to believe that he was the rankest kind of sucker—the greenest sort of country jake." Behind the uncouth manner and the weird mannerisms, however, was one of the shrewdest gamblers in America and an expert at the three-card monte. He was one of the few men who could show two aces and a queen and then, almost in the very act of throwing the cards, palm the queen and substitute a third ace.

He made enormous sums of money but, like so many others, lost it all ashore. While many professional gamblers were suckers for a particular game, Canada Bill was a sucker for them all. He would bet on anything and play any sort of game, and the fact that it was rigged made no difference to him. He loved gambling for gambling's sake. Legend had it that he was stuck for the night in some small river town, and after a diligent search, Bill found a faro game and began to play. His partner urged him to stop, warning him that the game was crooked. "I know it," Bill replied, "but it's the only game in town."

Canada Bill worked the riverboats until traffic on the Mississippi was stopped by the war. Afterward, he moved his activities to the railroads. A few years before his death, he actually offered one railroad a payment of $25,000 each year to allow him to operate a monte game on the line without being bothered. The offer was refused.

Bill died a pauper in 1880 in Reading, Pennsylvania, and was buried by the mayor of the city, who accepted donations from gamblers who had respected the old man. As two of the gamblers watched Bill's coffin being lowered into the ground, one of them offered to bet $1,000 to $500 that Canada Bill was not in the box. "Not with me," the other man replied. "I've known Bill to squeeze through tighter holes than that."

George Devol, unlike his friend Canada Bill, was more typical of the riverboat gamblers. He was one of the most important of the "sure-thing" players on the Mississippi, starting out as a professional cardsharp at age fifteen. Working as a cabin boy aboard a steamboat that was piloted by his cousin, he learned to cheat at an early age and had a bankroll of more than $3,000 within a year. It was a huge sum for such a young man to possess in those days, but at the end of fifty years as a gambler, he had little more to show for his time. He probably saw at least $2 million pass through his hands over the decades, but most of it ended up in faro banks in St. Louis, Chicago and New Orleans. With the exception of Canada Bill, he was probably the best monte player who ever trimmed the suckers on the steamboats. He was also skilled at cheating at poker and other card games, especially when he controlled the deck. But like so many other great players, he couldn't pass up the faro table and lost a fortune to hundreds of crooked games.

Much of Devol's fame on the river and in New Orleans was based on his abilities as a fighter. He once said that he probably had been in more rough-and-tumble fights than any man in America, and he was likely right. He always carried a pistol but never used it. He also seldom hit a man with his hands. In most encounters, he simply butted his opponent into submission with his head. With the weight of his burly, two-hundred-pound body behind it, his head was a formidable weapon. Several doctors who examined him at the height of his fame said that the skull above his forehead was more than an inch thick.

For several years during and after the Civil War, one of the attractions of the Robinson's Circus was Billy Carroll, who was advertised as the "man with the thick skull." In the center ring, Carroll smashed barrels and heavy doors with his head and would butt heads with all comers. He was never knocked down until the circus played New Orleans in the winter of 1867.

At the behest of several local sporting men, Carroll and Devol butted heads, just for fun. When the circus star regained consciousness, he walked over to Devol, put his hand on the gambler's head and laughed: "Gentlemen, I have found my papa at last."

Gambling did not exist in New Orleans merely on the riverboats that passed by the city; it was also the single greatest vice enjoyed by the Creole people of the region. "All indulge in it," wrote Claude C. Robin, a French visitor to New Orleans in the early 1800s. "In the evening, when the business day is over, fortunes are lost over and over again." The addiction to games of chance was so great, and so much a part of the Creole character, that legend had it that the first of the criminal colonists sent to Louisiana by the Mississippi Company came ashore with a deck of cards in his pocket and a roulette wheel under his arm. True or not, gambling was such a source of worry to the early government that Governor Bienville found it necessary to scold the settlers for wasting their time and substance with frivolous pursuits.

The first public houses in the city provided gaming tables for the convenience of their customers and operated games that were open to all comers. The provincial authorities attempted, without success, to abate the evil by issuing proclamations and creating stern regulations that promised punishments like branding, whipping, the stocks and, in extreme cases, banishment from the colony. It did little good. The people of New Orleans simply loved to gamble.

Gambling among the wealthy in the early days was private, but in later years most games could be found in special rooms that were hidden in high-class restaurants, ballrooms and coffeehouses. During the days of the French and Spanish rule, the city was still too isolated for establishments that were devoted strictly to gambling. They did not appear until after the Louisiana Purchase, when the settlement began to develop as a cosmopolitan city. By 1810, gambling houses were numerous, both in the French Quarter and in the new section above Canal Street. The houses became the focus of so much crime and disorder that the authorities attempted to control them over the course of the next sixty years by alternating systems of suppression, regulation and licensing by the state, which in later periods imposed a hefty annual tax.

The professional gambler was a rare character in early New Orleans, but once the region was opened to the riverboats, New Orleans became a favorite haunt for cardsharps. Vice areas sprang up to service the gamblers and the crews from the boats, and every establishment, even the bordellos, began offering games of chance, most of which were crooked.

Gambling in New Orleans was popular with just about every man in New Orleans, whether rich or poor, and almost every public house and tavern offered a gaming table and poker for their patrons. *Courtesy of the Library of Congress.*

According to one classic story, the only square game among the scores frequented by the riverboat men was found in a small roulette house on Tchoupitoulas Street. It was operated by a Frenchman named Grampin, who allegedly went bankrupt in a very strange fashion. Among his regular customers was a boat captain who came in every night that he was in New Orleans and bet twenty-five cents—never more and never less—on the red at roulette. One night, the captain sat down, placed his bet and leaned his head on his hand while Grampin spun the wheel. Red won, and the captain's money was doubled, but since he did not pick up his winnings, Grampin spun the wheel again. Once more, the ball stopped on red, and the old man's money doubled again. Again and again, the now nervous Grampin spun the wheel, while the riverboat captain sat motionless, apparently unconcerned about both his good fortune and the excitement that his winning streak was causing in the house. At the sixteenth turn of the wheel, when the captain's winnings amounted to more than $8,000 on an original investment of a quarter, Grampin pushed all of the money he had across the table at the old man and ordered him to leave. When the captain still didn't move, Grampin pushed him and the old man fell over on the floor—he was dead. With great speed, several members of his crew, who had accompanied him to the gambling house, gathered up the body and all of the winnings and rushed out of the place. Grampin had been bankrupted by a dead man!

The professional gamblers who operated in New Orleans, making it their permanent home, were drab fellows when compared to the gaudy sharps of the riverboats. Their dress and demeanor was indistinguishable from the average citizen. The only colorful gamblers in the city were those who came ashore for a brief respite from fleecing travelers on the river. For the first twenty-five years or so after the American annexation of New Orleans, the gambling houses were as plain and unpretentious as the local gamblers. They were usually small places on the side streets, fitted with roulette wheels and a few tables at which card games were played.

The first well-appointed "palace of chance," which became known as one of the finest places to lose money in the United States, was opened at Bourbon and Orleans Streets by John Davis in 1827. Davis was the owner of the famed Theatre d'Orleans and the Orleans Ballroom and had considerable social and political influence. The gambling house was open day and night, seven days a week, with croupiers and dealers working in four-hour shifts. It was beautifully decorated and offered a number of amenities, including a Sunday night dinner that was served free to all gamblers. Although Davis started this establishment at a time when gambling was being suppressed in the city, he was not bothered by the authorities. He had a monopoly on the trade until 1832, when the legislature legalized gambling in New Orleans and made it possible for anyone to open a gambling house for only an annual seventy-five-dollar fee. At that point, a number of other noted resorts appeared, including Hewlett's, Toussaint's and St. Cyr's on Chartres Street and Pradat's, Elkin's and Charton's on Canal Street.

In the public casinos of these establishments, there were about a dozen ways for a man to lose money, but the most popular methods were faro, roulette and blackjack. The proprietors, as Davis had done originally, provided smaller private rooms for the convenience of wealthy customers and public officials who didn't want to be seen gambling with the common people. Most of the private rooms were devoted to poker. There was no limit in the gambling houses of the time, and often the play was for very high stakes, especially in the private rooms. A loss of $25,000 or more in a single game

In the New Orleans casinos, there were about a dozen ways for a man to lose his money, but the most popular were poker, faro, blackjack and roulette. *Courtesy of the Library of Congress.*

was not uncommon, and many men of wealth won hundreds of thousands of dollars each year at games of chance. Others became destitute almost overnight, staking their plantations, their real estate in the city, their slaves and everything of value they owned. Members of the Marigny family were said to have gambled so heavily—and so poorly—that in order to pay their losses they were compelled to break up their famous plantation and sell a large part of the land as building plots. Perhaps the most consistent loser in New Orleans was John R. Grymes, the noted lawyer who acquired notoriety with his defense of Jean Lafitte. Grymes's law practice brought in a large income, but he gambled all of his money away and died a poor man. Tradition had it that although he gambled at every opportunity, he never won a hand, and for more than a decade his losses averaged more than $50,000 a year.

The fickle nature of the Louisiana legislature caused a repeal of the 1832 gambling laws just three years later, and in 1835, it became illegal to operate a gambling establishment. Owners of resorts faced fines up to $10,000 and imprisonment if arrested. Little attention was paid to the law in New Orleans, though, where public opinion was firmly in favor of gambling. Houses continued to operate with the cooperation of the police, although a little less openly than before. Unfortunately, nearly all of the better places, as well as the underworld spots, succumbed to the financial panics and depression of 1837. Gambling in the city languished for nearly ten years after.

In 1846, gambling was revived when New Orleans became the principal base of operations for the American army's foray into Mexico. It continued to be strong a few years later, when it became a departure point for many would-be gold prospectors who were on their way to California. Ships departed daily for Panama, where trains connected travelers to the ships traveling along the Pacific coast to the gold fields. With such a transient population coming to the city, gambling houses were opened on nearly every street, near the steamship landings, near the hotels and boardinghouses and just about anywhere that returning soldiers and departing prospectors gathered. No exact count of these establishments, which made no pretense toward luxury or elegance, was ever made, but it has been estimated that they numbered at least five hundred.

Most of the hastily opened halls closed down after the war with Mexico ended and the excitement over California started to subside. Gambling in New Orleans soon returned to normal proportions, only to see a revival of the luxury and splendor of the early days in the 1850s. It was at this time that Price McGrath, James Sherwood and Henry Perritt, who had successfully operated large establishments in St. Louis and other cities, arrived in New Orleans. They formed a partnership under the name McGrath & Company and acquired property on Carondelet Street, which they refurbished at a cost of more than $70,000. They opened a gambling house of such elegance and variety that it easily surpassed the earlier establishment of John Davis. It is said to have been the first resort of its kind in America where croupiers and dealers were required to wear evening dress. The elaborate dinners that were served each night were celebrated all over the country. In addition to being perhaps the most splendid gambling house in the country, it was also the most honest. No cheats were employed, and the partners tried to keep men who could not afford to lose away from the tables. The success of this policy influenced the dozen or so other large houses that were opened around the same time, and New Orleans enjoyed a few years of honest gaming.

Among the noted establishments that competed with McGrath & Company during this period were those operated by Augustus Lauraine and his partner, Charles Cassidy, and another opened by Sam Levy and Lorenzo Lewis, who was often known as Count Lorenzo because of the elegance of his apparel. The most exclusive house of the time was kept by a Frenchman named Curtius, located at Toulouse and Chartres Streets. No one was admitted without character references and a formal introduction by someone known to Curtius. Each player paid $0.50 an hour, which entitled him to dinner and as much wine as he wanted. The only games allowed were chess and poker, and at poker, there was a betting limit of $100.00 on a single hand.

All of the large houses ceased operations in 1861 when the Civil War began and the Confederate military authority largely assumed control of the city. Many of the riverboat gamblers abandoned their work on the Mississippi at the start of the war and sought refuge in New Orleans. With the gamblers who remained in the city, they formed a military company known as the Wilson Rangers, which was better known among the gamblers themselves as the Blackleg Cavalry. They equipped themselves with the best horses and weapons money could buy, but their gallantry was an illusion maintained to impress the people of the city. When ordered out to drill, they rode out of town and spent most of the day sleeping, playing cards and reading books on war tactics under a shade tree. They remained there until the cool of the evening, when they mounted their horses and returned to New Orleans. George Devol, the gambler and a member of the company, later wrote, "When we would get back into the city, the people would come out and cheer, wave handkerchiefs and present us with bouquets; for we had been drilling in the hot sun, preparing to protect their homes from the northern invaders…The citizens called us their defenders; and we did defend them, so long as there was no hostile foe within five hundred miles of them."

The gamblers' company was called into active service in April 1862 when David Farragut's Union fleet launched its attacks on the Confederate forts protecting New Orleans. They were sent down the river to engage a large Union land force that was reported to be marching on the city. "As we went marching down the street," Devol wrote, "the ladies presented us with bouquets and cheered us; but there was little cheer in that fine body of gamblers." The Rangers were about six miles below the city when one of the Union fired on them, sending the gamblers into a full retreat. Devol added: "When we got back to the city, we dismounted without orders, cut the buttons off our coats, buried our sabers and tried to make ourselves look as much like peaceful citizens as possible; for we had enough of military glory, and were tired of war."

On the morning of April 24, 1862, fire alarms throughout New Orleans alerted the residents that Farragut's ships had passed the forts and the city's defenses had fallen. Immediately, the city was thrown into a panic, for it was widely believed that New Orleans would be looted and burned by the invaders. Business was suspended, and thousands of people rushed to the levees to watch the conquering fleet as it steamed up the river. Governor Thomas O. Moore and other state and city officials prepared to flee, and General Mansfield Lovell, in command of the Confederate land forces, seized all available boats, loaded them with ordnance and military goods and dispatched them up the river to safety. He also issued orders to burn all of the cotton stored in the city, all of the shipyards and all of the steamers not needed by the Confederate army. Fifteen thousand bales of cotton were burned in the streets and on the levees. Steamboats that were at the docks, loaded with cotton, were set on fire and cast adrift.

In the midst of the preparations for evacuation, rioting and looting broke out. Soon, thousands of men and women were fighting for spoils of every kind, particularly for barrels of sugar and molasses and cases of meat. Confederate troops tried to calm the situation, but the people paid little attention to them. The looting continued until nearly everything on the levees had been carried away. The merchants in town expected the city to be sacked by the Northerners, so they threw open their doors and allowed people to take whatever they wanted.

New Orleans surrendered without a single shot being fired, and on May 1, 1862, Major General Benjamin F. Butler was placed in charge as the military governor of the city. He remained in that office until December 16, when he was recalled to Washington, but during those seven months, he managed to make himself the most hated man in New Orleans history.

Butler saw no need to be gentle in his position of power in New Orleans, and his methods earned him great scorn. He hanged a man suspected of desecrating the American flag, closed a secessionist newspaper and confiscated the property of anyone who would not swear allegiance to the Union. This was part of his first official act as governor, the Federal Confiscation Act. It allowed him to seize the property of any citizen of New Orleans who would not swear loyalty to the United States. As it turned out, Butler was little more than a run-of-the-mill corrupt politician, and he used his military authority to put money into his pockets and into those of friends and relatives, as well. His brother, A.J. Butler, made $2 million in New Orleans by nefarious means, including trading with the enemy, during the military occupation. Butler himself was said to have left

Major General Benjamin F. Butler managed to make himself one of the most hated men in New Orleans history by treating the people with disdain, issuing outrageous orders and plundering the wealth of the city for his own personal gain.

the stricken city with an even greater fortune, all taken during his "official" confiscations.

But this was not seen as Butler's greatest crime—that was Order No. 28. Before this order was issued, the women of New Orleans blatantly insulted Butler's men in the streets, calling them names. When one woman opened her window and emptied the contents of a chamber pot over Admiral David Farragut's head, Butler issued General Order No. 28. It simply stated that any woman who insulted a member of the United States Army would be treated from that point as a prostitute in the midst of plying her trade. The people of New Orleans, and throughout the South, were outraged by this unchivalrous and demeaning order, and Butler was labeled with the nickname of "Beast." However, he refused to back down, and the harassment of his men stopped. Incidentally, no woman was ever arrested. From that point on, the ladies had to resign themselves to hiring artists to paint the likeness of Butler on the bottom of their porcelain chamber pots.

Butler also issued two orders that had a direct effect on gambling in New Orleans. One, sent out through regular military channels, closed all of the gambling houses in the city. The second, circulated privately, permitted any gambler to reopen who would pay a license fee and accept Major General Butler's brother as a full, but silent, partner. Most of the establishments reopened under these terms, and from this source, A.J. Butler received huge sums of money every week. This continued until Major General Butler was called back to Washington and his enterprises collapsed.

Butler's military successors left the gamblers alone, and they enjoyed prosperity for nearly two years. Since all of the gamblers were Southern, they took great delight in fleecing the officers and soldiers of the Federal army. Despite warnings and a few punishments, New Orleans's gamblers so depleted the Union army's funds that early in 1864, all of the gambling houses in the city were closed down. They remained closed, under strict observation, until the military eventually left New Orleans and Louisiana fell into the clutches of the carpetbaggers.

In 1868, another form of gambling came to New Orleans when the Louisiana legislature chartered a state lottery to a group that agreed to pay $40,000 toward the operation of the Charity Hospital. The lottery operators offered a $600,000 prize, minus the hospital proceeds, and a $15,000 slush fund to pay off state legislators to go along with it. When the deal was in danger of failing in 1877, Confederate generals Jubal Early and P.G.T. Beauregard were hired to appear in full dress uniforms to conduct the weekly drawings. The federal government finally shut down the lottery in 1895 and prosecuted all of the officials who were involved.

In New Orleans, gambling houses were not generally reopened until 1869, when a new and corrupt civil legislature passed a law to legalize gambling—and levy a tax of $5,000 on each house.

At the time when gambling was legalized once again, New Orleans had a population of about 200,000 people, largely made up of carpetbaggers who had amassed wealth by exploiting the city and state, and was able to support more gambling houses than at any time in its history. When the opportunity arose, local gamblers opened their doors, and sharps from all over the United States flocked to the city, where their business was not only legitimate but was also free from all inspection and supervision. Many of the new houses paid the required tax, but an equal number of them avoided it and remained open through the assistance of bribed police officials.

Within a few weeks after the passage of the law, New Orleans had been transformed into "gambling hell." Games of every description, most of them crooked, ran wide-open on all of the principal streets of the French Quarter and the section above Canal Street. On St. Charles Avenue alone, between city hall and Canal Street, there were forty resorts—referred to as the "forty thieves"—that never closed their doors. Many were opened in three-story buildings with faro on the first floor, roulette on the second and poker on the third. Separate rooms offered private games on every floor. The front doors of these places opened directly onto the street, and the sidewalks swarmed with barkers who tried to lure men inside and with shell and monte men who worked openly, not bothered by the police. At the same time, a plague of confidence men invaded the hotels, railroad stations and steamboat landings in a bold search for victims.

But the law that the gamblers had greeted with such enthusiasm proved to be their undoing. Within six months, so many resorts had been opened by strangers that the old-time honest gamblers of New Orleans found themselves facing financial ruin. Their carefully built reputations for honest games had been destroyed by the excess of sure-thing operators. Under the leadership of Bill Franklin, who ran a place at Common Street and St. Charles Avenue, a conference was held, and the veteran gamblers decided that, whatever the cost, the newcomers had to be driven out of the city. A committee was appointed, funds were collected and some of the best-known gamblers in the city began working for a repeal of the law that had legalized their profession. They were successful, and by the end of the next legislative session, the license system was abolished and gambling in New Orleans was once again illegal. The larger houses were closed for a few weeks while the police, with whom satisfactory arrangements had been made, rid the city of the undesirables. A short time later, the big houses opened again, and for the next decade, the gamblers operated quietly and with great prosperity, in spite of the huge bribes paid out to the police and public officials.

In the late 1870s, though, the sure-thing men returned to New Orleans, and the French Quarter was once more awash in cheap gambling parlors and three-card monte operators. In 1881, a new plan was concocted to try to control gambling in the city. It was called the "Shakespeare Plan," named for Mayor Joseph Shakespeare, and it was probably the only system ever devised in America, with the exception of outright suppression, that succeeded in keeping the activities of gamblers within bounds.

When Shakespeare assumed office in late 1880, there were eighty-three large gambling houses in New Orleans. He was in favor of licensing a limited number of resorts and closing the rest, but the city council refused to pass the needed ordinance, pointing out that the State of Louisiana had banned gambling and that crime could not be licensed. The mayor then decided to try regulating gambling his own way.

Early in 1881, the gamblers were told that their establishments would be closed at the first complaint, and less than a month later, after the fleecing of a visiting French nobleman caused a sensation in the newspapers, the police closed every gambling house in the city except those in the area bounded by Camp, Chartres, St. Louis, Bourbon, Carondelet and Gravier Streets, where the most important establishments were located. The mayor then called a meeting with these operators and presented his plan to them. He suggested that they pay him a fixed sum each month, and in return, he would make sure that they were not bothered or extorted by the police. He further promised that they would not be prosecuted and that no competing houses would be allowed to open. For their part, the gamblers had to promise to run honest games, to restrict entry to their houses to adults and to follow whatever rules the mayor set up.

The plan was a success from the beginning. Most of the payments made to the mayor were applied to the construction and upkeep of the Shakespeare Almshouse, a project for the poor, and the rest was used for the maintenance of a small force of private detectives whose only duties were to inspect the gambling houses at regular intervals and see that the games were conducted honestly.

The Shakespeare Plan remained in effect throughout the administration of successors W.J. Behan and J. Valsin Guillotte. About 1885, though, politicians and city officials, anxious to increase payments that were by now being siphoned off in all directions, permitted several crooked gamblers to open houses. The diversion of the funds away from the poorhouse eventually resulted in a scandal that was widely reported in the newspapers. Grand jury indictments followed, and the reputation of the plan was destroyed.

Shakespeare tried to reinstate the plan when he became mayor again in 1888, but by then it was too late. The gamblers, burned by the corrupt politicians, refused to have any part of it. In the end, the mayor was forced to fall back on the system of control that became commonly used in New Orleans and other American cities—look the other way until the gamblers become too bold, then carry out raids and prosecutions until they go back underground again. Out of sight, as far as illegal gambling went, was out of the public mind.

But gambling never really lost its popularity in New Orleans. Stories say that in the 1930s, notorious Senator Huey Long allowed mobster Frank Costello to install slot machines in the city in return for a contribution to the "widows and orphans fund."

In the 1940s, it was said that there were no open gambling establishments in New Orleans proper but that "in Jefferson Parish, the temples of luck seem to outnumber the temples of God." Several of these "temples of luck" were extremely popular and advertised the fact that they were just minutes away from downtown New Orleans.

One such establishment was the Southport Club, which was said to be owned by local boss Carlos Marcello. Another, more famous place was the Beverly Country Club, which in addition to being operated by Marcello, was also owned by Frank Costello and famed mobster Meyer Lansky. The club opened in 1945, offering illegal gambling and headliners like Danny Thomas, Rudy Vallee and a number of other popular entertainers and celebrities. In the early 1950s, a Senate investigative committee came to New Orleans to look into exactly what was being offered at the Beverly. Not long after, it was closed down. The club did reopen again in 1972 as a dinner theatre only but closed again in 1983 when the building burned down.

The years following World War II led to a crackdown on gambling, and dozens of establishments were closed. It would not be until 1991 that legal gambling came back to the city with passage of legislation allowing a lottery, riverboat gambling and a single land-based casino.

"HELL ON EARTH"

NEW ORLEANS CRIME AND VICE

As New Orleans began to grow into a real American city in the mid-1800s, crime of every description began to increase. With money and more wealth flowing into the city, the underworld grew rich and powerful. During the twenty years before the Civil War, and for an even longer period after, the newspapers were almost constantly filled with reports of robberies, assaults and murders. The New Orleans correspondent for the *New York Tribune* wrote in January 1855 that "murders here are an everyday occurrence and the papers daily give details of the same. A thousand murders might be committed in New Orleans, and if the murderers could not be found on the spot, our authorities would never afterward make any effort to have them punished." The city, the newspapers said, was suffering under a "reign of terror."

By the late 1850s, newspapers reported that inquests were being held for as many as two murdered persons each week and that it was common knowledge that at least two-thirds of the homicides committed in the underworld districts were never reported to the police and the bodies of the victims were never found. In 1861, the criminal sheriff of the Orleans Parish was quoted as saying that the place was a "perfect hell on earth" and that "nothing could put an end to the murders, manslaughters, and deadly assaults till it was made penal to carry arms." No permit was required for the possession of firearms in those days, and men of all classes habitually carried weapons to protect their lives and property.

Criminals and ruffians had turned New Orleans into what the criminal sheriff colorfully described as "hell on earth." Outlaws and lawbreakers

During the mid-1800s, New Orleans had become what the sheriff of Orleans Parish called "a perfect hell on earth," thanks to the crime and violence on the streets.

found refuge in scores of cheap taverns, dance houses, bordellos, concert saloons and barrelhouses, with which the French Quarter and the area above Canal Street were infested. Probably no other city in the United States was home to as many unsavory resorts in proportion to its number of citizens. On St. Charles Avenue alone, between Canal Street and Lafayette Square, there were forty-five places where liquor was sold, and nearly all of them were disreputable. Similar congestions of underworld spots appeared in other places, notably along Gallatin Street in the French Quarter and on Girod Street in the American section. Even in neighborhoods where grocery stores outnumbered taverns, the stores still managed to sell more whiskey than food.

BARRELHOUSES AND CONCERT SALOONS

Almost every conceivable type of establishment that offered vice had been common in New Orleans since the start of the colony, and the number of those places kept up with the growth of the city and the increase in population. However, the barrelhouse and the concert saloon were products of the Civil War era. Both were introduced to New Orleans by disreputable northerners who flocked to the city in the wake of the Union army's invasion. They served to add their particular talents and appetites to the criminal element that already formed a large and dangerous part of the population.

The barrelhouse was one of the lowest forms of liquor establishments in American history. It was strictly a drinking place that usually occupied a long, narrow room with a row of racked barrels on one side. On the other side of the room was a table with large glass tumblers or earthenware mugs stacked on it. For five cents, a customer was permitted to fill a mug or tumbler at the spigot of any of the barrels, but if he failed to refill almost immediately he was promptly thrown out to make room for another patron. Drinking in a barrelhouse was meant to be done quickly and with the single goal of getting drunk. Once he was barely able to stand, the customer was taken out into the alley, or a back room, and usually robbed.

Most of these seedy dives served only brandy, whiskey and wine, although the liquors that masqueraded under these names barely passed for palatable. A barrel of neutral spirits became "Irish whiskey" when a half-pint of creosote was dumped into it. The wine was simply three parts water and one part alcohol with coloring and flavor added. Brandy was usually manufactured by taking a half barrel of water and adding grape juice, a pound of burned sugar, a half-ounce of sulphuric acid and a plug of chewing tobacco for a little kick. Then the barrel was filled the rest of the way with neutral spirits.

Another ingredient frequently added to all of the mixtures was knockout drops, by which the owner of the barrelhouse was ensured that he would end up with all of the customer's money, not just some of it. Such men not only doped the liquor but also maintained a staff of thieves who relieved the drunks of their money and all of their clothing, as well. The thieves usually worked on a percentage basis and took turns robbing the unlucky wretches who made the mistake of walking into a barrelhouse in the first place.

The concert saloon was a step up from the dingy and dirty barrelhouses. As a forerunner of the modern nightclub, they provided a dance floor for patrons who wanted to dance and listen to the music of a tinny piano or a screeching fiddle. Occasional shows were also provided on small stages without curtains or scenery, and plenty of food and drink was served by young women, popularly known as "beer jerkers," who also doubled as dancers and singers. The first resort of this kind opened its doors on St. Charles Avenue about 1865. It became so popular that others soon followed. Over the next twenty years, about fifteen such establishments came to the city. They employed between one hundred and two hundred beer jerkers, the number varying by just how popular the place became. The girls received no salaries but were allowed to keep whatever tips they received and were paid a 10 percent commission on beer sales. From these sources, the girls usually made about twenty-five to thirty dollars a week, which they added to by working as prostitutes on the side.

The entertainment at the concert saloon, which was in addition to the girl waiters, generally consisted of girls dancing the cancan, which was considered quite risqué at the time, and "art poses by living models," in

Concert saloons offered entertainment to the drinkers who were expected to buy drinks from the "beer jerkers," who also worked as prostitutes in the establishments. Men who drank too much could usually expect to be robbed.

which female performers wore ankle-length, form-fitting cotton tights with long sleeves. The shows must have been much worse than they seemed from their description. On June 18, 1869, after a dozen "actresses" from a concert saloon had been fined $1 each and the owners of two establishments were placed under bonds of $250 to keep the peace for six months, a piece in the *New Orleans Times* read: "We can state that in an experience of some years we have never observed in any of the dance-houses of Gallatin or Barracks Street, or the ballrooms of the demi-monde further downtown, the utter abandon which has characterized these places."

The St. Nicholas was the first concert saloon to open in New Orleans, but it was followed by the Napoleon, the Bismarck, the Pavilion, the Gem, the Royal Palace Beer Saloon & Concert Hall, the Conclave, the Buffalo Bill House and Wenger's Garden on Bourbon Street, which in 1869 proudly summoned patrons to inspect a novelty that was advertised as "the remarkable machine known as the self-acting organ."

Other such establishments had their own claims to fame. At the Conclave, it was the garish decorations; the "wine-room," where aerated cider was sold as champagne; the life-size portrait of Don Quixote in the entrance lobby; and the spectacle of the proprietor, dressed as Cervante's character, lurking about the place keeping order with a large wooden club. The Conclave was one of the few places to keep a bar in addition to table service, and the arrangement of the bar back created quite a disturbance in the city. It was an exact replica of the burial vaults, or ovens, which spanned a wall of St. Louis Cemetery No. 1. The marble slabs, instead of bearing the names of the dead, were chiseled with "brandy, whiskey, gin, etc." The bartenders were dressed as undertakers, and when one of them served a customer, he opened a vault in the bar and pulled out a small, silver-handled casket lined with bottles of the liquor the patron ordered. The Conclave was a popular drinking spot for the tourist crowd, but it never really caught on with the dedicated drinkers.

The Royal Palace Beer Saloon & Concert Hall was operated by Otto Henry Schoenhausen. He opened the resort in 1867, but it was closed down two years later when Schoenhausen went to prison for the murder of Dr. H.L. Nelson in a Canal Street confectionary. He was pardoned by the governor in 1882 and came out of the penitentiary with $10,000, which he had acquired by lending money to the guards at high interest rates. He immediately reopened the Royal Palace, and for the next seven or eight years it was one of the most popular—and disreputable—resorts in the city. Schoenhausen employed about twenty waiter girls, some of whom also sang and danced, and sold beer for five cents a glass and forty cents a bottle.

The Buffalo Bill House was kept by a scruffy, bearded ruffian named Bison Williams, who came to New Orleans from Cincinnati in the latter part of 1862 and ran a lunchroom on St. Charles Avenue until the end of the Civil War. He then opened his combination concert saloon and dance house and installed a staff of leg-breakers and prostitutes to handle and service his customers. He scorned the "art poses by living models" that were popular at other such resorts and instead offered his patrons bare-knuckle boxing, head-butting contests, wrestling matches and rat and dog fights. For those not looking for blood sports, his cancan dancers and performers performed indecent song and dance acts.

Bison Williams's most popular butters were two underworld characters known as Looney and Oyster Johnny, who bashed each other bloody three times each week throughout the summer of 1869. They knocked each other senseless for a promised purse of fifty dollars. By the end of the summer, Oyster Johnny was finally proclaimed the top man. After forty-five minutes of "sport," Looney was finally knocked unconscious. But when Johnny tried to collect the purse that he had been working to win for months, Bison Williams denied any knowledge of the cash. He gave Johnny a bottle of headache pills and a stiff drink and then kicked him out.

Almost from the time Williams opened his joint, it was a favorite for the most unsavory members of the New Orleans underworld. For just that reason, it was the toughest and most dangerous of the concert saloons. By late 1869, it had become so notorious that several newspapers denounced it as a nuisance and demanded that the police close it down. Bison Williams shrugged off the complaints about the fights and robberies and replied that he had purposely opened the place "in the only locality in the city where decent people do not live."

For several years, the Buffalo Bill House was the headquarters of a number of well-known local criminals, including Pierre Bertin and Jean Capdeville, New Orleans's most celebrated burglars. It was also a favorite haunt of Sam Gorman, an innocuous-looking old gentleman who was actually one of the slickest confidence men in the country and an accomplished burglar. Gorman was a New Yorker who spent his winters in New Orleans, and after his arrival each fall, the city always saw a sharp increase in the number of retail robberies and home invasions. When he was finally arrested in 1869—and released a few days later for lack of evidence—he was more than seventy years old and suffering from tuberculosis. He was a very wealthy man by this time, having extensive real estate holdings in New York. When a policeman asked him why he continued his life of crime, given that he was in poor health and rich enough to retire, the old man simply replied: "Well, it's fun."

Bertin and Capdeville planned many of their robberies at a table in the corner of the Buffalo Bill House and also openly displayed samples of homemade burglary tools for sale to other would-be thieves. They also made simple weapons for street robbers, the most popular being a "slung-shot," which was a heavy piece of rope with a loop at one end and a chunk of lead at the other. It was brutally effective when knocking a victim over the head and stealing his cash. For pickpockets, they made large finger rings with tiny knife blades embedded in the settings. With these, the thieves could cut their victims' pockets. For more than a decade, Bertin and Capdeville carried out their various criminal enterprises, and although they were known to the police and frequently arrested, they were not successfully prosecuted until 1871. A jury found them guilty of "robbery with weapons," which in Louisiana in those days was a capital offense. The two men could have been hanged, but they were sentenced to life in prison instead. After a few months at the penitentiary, Bertin was pardoned by Governor H.C. Warmoth, but the pardon was withdrawn and he was returned to prison when the governor discovered that the signatures on the petition to get him released were forged.

The bawdy entertainment, the fights and the robberies that occurred in the concert saloons, together with the noise that accompanied these activities, finally drew so much ire from the newspapers and from civic groups that by 1870, the city finally attempted to drive them out of business. An ordinance was enacted that imposed heavy license fees on concert saloons, charging various amounts for musical instruments that were played and stage shows that were performed. Even if the owner of the establishment was willing to pay, he still had to obtain a waiver from the owners or tenants of nearby locations that proved they permitted the noise. A few of the resort owners closed their doors rather than pay the fee, but most paid without protest, and if they couldn't get the necessary signatures from nearby homes or establishments, they simply moved their operation to a part of the city that would allow it. Concert saloons remained a disreputable feature of New Orleans nightlife until about 1890, when they died of disinterest and a changing public taste in entertainment.

NEW ORLEANS'S ORIGINAL VICE DISTRICT

Gallatin Street in the French Quarter was New Orleans's first real vice district. Only two blocks long, stretching from Ursuline Avenue to Barracks, the street is no longer in existence today but was once located directly behind

Gallatin Street was New Orleans's first true vice district. The rough saloons and dance houses along this stretch of broken cobblestone street, only two blocks long, operated from sundown to sunrise every day. *Courtesy of the New Orleans Public Library.*

where the U.S. Mint now stands. For many years, this was the location of the old, weather-beaten warehouses of the French Market, but before that, it was the most dangerous place in the city. A policeman who was foolish enough to walk down Gallatin Street alone usually became a casualty or a missing person. The police quickly learned to handle complaints in this area in well-armed groups—and only in the daytime.

From about 1840 to the mid-1870s, the short stretch of rundown buildings and broken cobblestones that made up Gallatin Street saw more blood, violence and death than just about every other section of the city combined. During this era, there was not a single legitimate business on the street. It was completely filled with barrelhouses, dance houses that also served as bordellos, regular taverns, gambling parlors and boardinghouses from which sailors were occasionally shanghaied into service. From dawn

until dusk, the district slept off its debaucheries from the night before behind closed shutters, but after the sun went down, the doors opened on a raucous party that lasted all night long. The street was filled each night with locals, travelers, soldiers, sailors and steamboat men seeking women and every kind of vice imaginable.

And, in return, these men were being sought by the harlots, the thieves, the killers, the garrotters who openly carried their strangling cords and the foot pads who walked about with their "slung-shots" looped about their wrists. There was crime and depravity along every inch of Gallatin Street.

While Gallatin Street was inhabited by all sorts of dangerous characters, the worst bunch was the gang known as the Live Oak Boys. They were named for the menacing wooden cudgels that they carried and for the fact that, when not carousing in the district, they could be found lounging in the shade of a big pile of live oak knees (curved pieces of load-bearing wood using in ship construction) at a shipyard near the river. Once during the early days of the gang, the owner of the shipyard tried to get them off his property by moving the knees, but the gang threatened to burn them if he didn't move them back. The lumber remained in the same spot for the next twenty years, the recognized headquarters of the Live Oak Boys.

The gang, of which each member was a thief, a killer or a drunk, was founded by Red Bill Wilson in 1858. Wilson was a notorious resident of Gallatin Street who had a beard that was so thick and gnarled that he actually hid a knife inside it. Wilson may have started the gang, but it had no leader and no organization to it. There was no division of loot, and when it came to crime, each man was on his own and kept whatever he stole. If the occasion arose, they even robbed and killed one another. They were simply a loose confederation of men who did whatever they pleased. It was doubtful that a single one of them ever did an honest day's work. They devoted their nights to thieving and murder or to drinking and whoring on Gallatin Street. Their days were set aside for loafing, sleeping and planning new crimes.

For years, the Live Oak Boys were hated and feared by dance house proprietors. There was not a night that went by that they didn't raid one of the establishments on the street. Sometimes they broke a place up because they had been paid to do so by one of the owner's rivals, but on other occasions, they did it just because they loved a good brawl. When they came rushing into an establishment, their wooden clubs in hand, the bouncers, bartenders, musicians and customers ran out the back door. The gang would then wreck the place at their leisure, smash all of the furniture and musical instruments, rob the till and carry out as much liquor as they wanted. There were a few occasions when the owner of the place resisted the Live Oak Boys, but he usually didn't live to regret such a mistake.

Thanks to this kind of behavior, the Live Oak Boys weren't welcome anywhere in the Gallatin Street district except at the Fireproof Coffee House on Levee Street, which was owned by Bill Swan, a former gang member who had earned enough money to start his own business. The Live Oak Boys took his resort under their protection, partly because he was a friend and mostly because he let them drink for free. Because of this, the Fireproof was the most orderly spot in the neighborhood. Swan operated the place with great success until 1877, when he sold it and opened a saloon at Peters Street and Esplanade Avenue. At the new location, he expanded into dog fighting and rat killing, which were then popular "sports."

Aside from Bill Swan, most of the Live Oaks Boys died violently or ended up in prison. One of the gang members, Charley Lagerbeer, was regarded as the fiercest fighter of the lot. He was short and thickset with a bullet-shaped head and massive shoulders. He was shot by a saloonkeeper named Keppler, whom he killed, and he died in Charity Hospital. Another member, Hugh O'Brien, was killed when he tried to steal a rowboat from a fisherman on the river. His sons, Matt and Hugh Jr., were also members of the gang and got involved in a bloody argument in Bill Swan's old saloon in October 1886. The quarrel took place between the O'Briens while they were drinking with their brother-in-law, Johnny Hackett, and Jack Lyons, a ruffian who had been around Gallatin Street for years. Hackett and Lyons tried to stop the brothers from fighting, but when Matt continued to abuse his brother, Hackett handed Hugh a knife and told him to shut Matt up with it. The sight of the knife worked, at least temporarily. Matt O'Brien immediately stopped fighting when he saw it, and after a few more drinks, the brothers left the tavern, apparently on good terms. They walked together into Gallatin Street and then stopped and talked for a moment. Matt was seen to draw a pistol from his coat, and then he shot his brother in the side.

"Hughey was drunk," Matt told the police when he was arrested a few hours later. "He was going to do me up, and I shot him to keep him from doing it. I didn't give him no cause, only he was drunk and wanted blood."

Hugh O'Brien was not seriously hurt in the incident, and he left New Orleans to avoid having to testify against his brother. Regardless, Matt was charged with "assault less than mayhem" and was sentenced to the penitentiary.

The O'Brien brothers were some of the last dregs of the old gang. With one of them gone and the other in prison, there were only about a half-dozen Live Oak Boys still around. Most were old men by the late 1880s and, except for Bill Swan, had become aging barflies who spent most of their time in the gutter or looking for free drinks. Perhaps the worst of the remaining bunch was Crazy Bill Anderson, who had earned his nickname because of the enthusiasm that he had for fighting when he was a young man. He was arrested for drunkenness several times each month by 1886 and eventually died in jail.

THE WOMEN OF GALLATIN STREET

The dance houses of Gallatin Street operated in much the same way as the concert saloons that were scattered about in other questionable parts of the city, with the main attraction being dancing, liquor and loose women. What really set the houses of Gallatin Street apart was the fact that they were even lower on the scale of depravity than those found in other sections of New Orleans.

Each of the Gallatin Street houses was very much alike. A typical dance house occupied a two- or three-story building, with the upper floors sectioned off into small rooms that were rented by the night to streetwalkers or by the week to the prostitutes on the staff. All rents were payable in advance. According to a newspaper reporter who toured one of these establishments in 1869, the chambers were equipped "with furniture of the oldest and craziest patterns…and were filthy and unclean to a degree which beggars description."

The first floor of the place was divided into two rooms, and in one corner, on high stools, sat the bouncers, usually two or three rough bruisers armed with clubs, knives and brass knuckles on both hands. Ordinary fights, and even murders, didn't concern these men, as long as the fighters or killers dragged their victims outside into the street and didn't do their business inside the house. The bouncers quickly unleashed their fury on anyone who dared to damage property. The back room of the place was the dance hall, where music was produced by a piano, banjo, fiddle or perhaps a trumpet or trombone or two. No fee was charged for admission or dancing, but a man was expected to buy a drink for his girl after every dance. Whiskey, the liquor of choice, was sold for twenty cents a glass, but only the first two or three were served at full strength. After that, they were freely watered down so that a man wouldn't get too drunk to dance. If he did, he was robbed and then thrown out.

The women were the real draw to customers who came to the dance house, although these low-class drunkards and prostitutes could only have been appealing to the most desperate of men. They were a rough bunch that, as a general rule, wore their hair loose, badly worn slippers on their feet and knee-length calico dresses with nothing underneath. From ten to thirty such women were generally attached to a particular dance house, and additional women were brought in from the street or a nearby bordello when business was especially brisk. On such occasions, wrote a reporter for the *New Orleans Times* in 1869,

> *The long dance hall would be filled with some two or three hundred scowling, black-bearded, red-shirted visitors coming from every port, prison and lazar-house, and presenting such a motley throng as Lafitte or any of his pirates of the Gulf might have gathered for their crews. With a piano or two or three trombones for an orchestra, and with dances so abandoned and reckless that the can-can in comparison seemed maidenly and respectable, one can form an idea of what the scene was.*

The same reporter described the women at one of the dance houses as being "in an awful state of nudity" but failed to provide any details about what he meant. Such a state, however, was not uncommon on Gallatin Street. Excited by the dancing and the large amounts of liquor poured down their throats, they frequently took off their dresses and frolicked about naked. Many of the men quickly followed their example. On numerous occasions, it became necessary to stop the music and for the bouncers to clear the floor of couples who were doing everything but dancing. Such activities were normally confined to the upstairs of the house or, most often, the back alley.

None of the women received any sort of pay from the owners of the dance houses. The money they made was from tips, prostitution and whatever they could steal. However, a woman attached to a dance house was never without a willing companion for the night, or for the day either, since these operations kept their doors open around the clock. The men who did spend time with them were almost always robbed. And there was nothing subtle about a dance house harlot's methods. If a man was drunk, she simply emptied his pockets. If he wasn't, she used other means of getting to his money.

There was probably no method of robbery as effective as that employed against a man who came into Archie Murphy's resort in March 1859 and boasted to one of the house strumpets, Lizzie Collins, that he had $110 in gold bound to his leg with a handkerchief. He refused to drink but quickly accepted when Lizzie invited him upstairs. As they entered her darkened room, three other women jumped on him and knocked him to the floor while Lizzie poured whiskey down his throat. He could either swallow or drown, so he drank until he was sick and helplessly drunk. Lizzie then relieved him of the gold and summoned the bouncers from downstairs to throw the man out into the alley. The man later complained to the police, and the four women were brought into court. He was unable to prove any of his claims, though, and the charges were dismissed.

Oddly, Lizzie Collins developed a strange habit a year or so later that turned out to be her undoing. Instead of stealing money from the men she brought to her room, she waited until they were asleep and then cut the buttons off their pants and hid them away. In time, she had a great number of buttons but no money to pay her rent. Archie Murphy kicked her out, and she eventually turned to streetwalking and died a short time later. She was never able to explain her weird mania for buttons, and the tale of Lizzie's buttons was often told on Gallatin Street.

Another of Archie Murphy's girls was Mary Jane Jackson, a voluptuous young woman with a full head of blazing red hair that earned her the nickname of "Bricktop." There was no tougher woman on Gallatin Street, and she was probably ferocious enough to whip any man, even the worst of the Live Oak Boys. She never lost a fight, and in her eight-year career in the bordellos and dance houses of New Orleans, she killed four men and stabbed and beat scores of others.

Bricktop Jackson was born in the slums of the city in 1836 and became a product of her environment. By age thirteen, she was a prostitute, and at fourteen she was in fairly comfortable circumstances as the mistress of a Poydras Street bartender. She lived with him for three years, but eventually, he grew tired of her and kicked her out—much to his regret. When Bricktop found herself locked out of his house, she stormed into the bar where he worked and gave him a terrible beating. It landed him in the hospital, missing one ear and most of his nose. Bricktop then went to work on a bordello on Dauphine Street, and while she was popular with most of the men, thanks to her good looks and lush figure, she kept the house in such turmoil that after a few weeks, she was turned out into the street. She ended up being discharged from another half dozen brothels for the same reason, but in 1865, she went down to Gallatin Street and got a job at Archie Murphy's dance house.

Bricktop was the scourge of Gallatin Street for almost a year and a half. During that time, she committed two of her murders. She beat one man to death with a club and stabbed to death a man known as Long Charley, who stood almost seven feet tall in his socks. Bricktop used her favorite knife to do him in—a creation of her own design with five-inch blades at both ends and a center handgrip made from German silver. With this deadly weapon clutched in her fist, she could cut, slash and stab in any direction. It made her a person to be greatly feared, and this was probably the reason that she only remained at Archie Murphy's for a few weeks. Murphy threw her out and so did a few other dance houses operators who mistakenly thought they could tame her. Bricktop proved to be too tough even for Gallatin Street.

In late 1857, Bricktop became a freelance prostitute and worked as a thief and pickpocket while living in a small house on Dauphine Street with three other women whose combative personalities had also caused them to be barred from the Gallatin Street dance houses. The three women were a small but fierce girl named Ellen Collins; America Williams, who was six feet tall and stronger than most men; and Delia Swift, a fiery redhead like Bricktop who was better known as Bridget Fury. As Bricktop had done, Bridget started young and entered a life of crime at age twelve, working at a Cincinnati dance house where her father was a fiddler. She was still a child when she killed a girl and was sent to the Ohio state prison. After she was released, Bridget moved to New Orleans and got into as much trouble as Bricktop. In 1858, she murdered a man in the Poydras Street Market and was sentenced to life in prison.

Bricktop Jackson committed her third murder about a year after Bridget went to jail. On November 7, 1859, along with Ellen Collins and America Williams, she went to Joe Seidensahl's beer garden and began drinking. At the table next to them was Laurent Fleury, one of Seidensahl's boarders, eating lunch. Bricktop picked up a knife, and when Fleury told her to put it down, she swore at him and threatened to cut out his heart with it. Fleury, who undoubtedly did not recognize Bricktop, slapped her across the face, which caused all three women to attack him, screaming with rage. Seidensahl came to Fleury's assistance, but he was unarmed, and the women, knives in hand, drove the men out into the backyard. Seidensahl was seriously wounded in the attack, and Fleury was stabbed six times. He died three days later. One of Seidensahl's employees shot at the women from an upstairs window, but they threw pieces of brick at him until he ducked for cover. Ellen Collins escaped before the police arrived, but Bricktop and America were arrested. They were acquitted because the coroner, under whose direction a very flimsy postmortem examination was made, was unable to say under oath what killed Fleury. Bricktop's lawyer claimed that the man had died from heart disease.

While she was in the parish prison awaiting her trial, Bricktop fell in love with one of the prison turnkeys, a man named John Miller, who was little better than a criminal himself. Miller was born in Gretna and for several years was the manager and handler of prizefighters. In 1854, he was managing a heavyweight named Charley Keys, who had defeated every opponent on the Gretna side of the Mississippi. A match was arranged with Tom Murray, a noted brawler from Gallatin Street, and the men met for a bout. Keys was being beaten, so Miller attacked Murray's manager with a knife. A fight ensued, and Miller's left arm was so badly cut that it had to be amputated. When the stump healed, he fastened a chain to it and often went about with an iron ball the size of a fist attached to the end of the chain. With a knife in his remaining hand and the iron ball whirling above his head, Miller was a terrifying sight during a brawl. He was the undisputed ruler of Gretna until early in 1857, when he came to New Orleans and killed a man in a fight. He was sentenced to two years in the parish prison, and after serving his term, he was, for reasons that seem inexplicable, given a job as a prison guard.

When Bricktop was released after the charges of murdering Laurent Fleury were dropped, Miller resigned his job, and the two moved into Miller's shack in Freetown. They lived there for almost two years of constant unhappiness, occasionally swapping their domestic brawls for trips to Gallatin Street, where the pair proved to be a match for even the toughest dance house bouncers. They continued to fight on a daily basis until October 1861, when Bricktop slashed Miller with her knife and returned to New Orleans. Miller followed and begged her to come back to him. Bricktop gave in and returned to Freetown.

On December 5, 1861, Miller came home with a cowhide whip and told Bricktop that she needed a good thrashing. She promptly took the whip away from him and beat him mercilessly. Bruised and bloodied, he tried to brain her with the iron ball, but she seized it in midair and dragged the man to her by his chain. Frantic with fear and anger, Miller pulled a knife, but Bricktop snatched it from his hand, slammed him against the wall and then held him by the throat as she stabbed him five times in the belly and chest. He was dead when she let him fall to the floor.

Bricktop was sent to jail for Miller's murder, but both she and Bridget Fury were released in September 1862 when the military governor of the state, General George F. Shepley, nearly emptied the penitentiary by issuing blanket pardons. Bricktop never returned to New Orleans, but Bridget was a familiar figure for almost another decade. She opened a brothel on Dryades Street in 1869, but a week or two later, two customers were robbed there and Bridget and five of her girls were hauled into court. She served five months in jail for her part in the theft, and by the time she was released, her bordello had been taken over by a competitor. Within a year she was a broken woman, sleeping in gutters and being arrested regularly for drunkenness. Like so many others of her sort, she died in poverty.

FROM BASIN STREET
TO STORYVILLE

PROSTITUTION IN NEW ORLEANS

The image of New Orleans as the most exciting city in America was created by the ballrooms, restaurants, hotels, coffeehouses, elegant gambling halls and unrestrained festivity of Mardi Gras and Carnival. But the fact that at the same time the city was known throughout the country as a cesspool of sin and vice was principally due to prostitution in New Orleans, which in turn was due to the tolerance with which it was regarded by the authorities and the local populace. This attitude, which was eagerly embraced by politicians since it provided one of the main sources of graft, was based on the belief that prostitution was a necessary evil. It should be regulated, most believed, not suppressed. Prostitution was big business, and because so many profited from it, officials were adamant about keeping it in the city.

Prostitution had always been a part of New Orleans, from the arrival of the first colonists, many of whom were part of what has been called the world's oldest profession. In the years that followed the Louisiana Purchase, the demand for prostitution in the city grew as women were needed to service the crews of the flatboats and steamships on the Mississippi River. Vice was confined during this time to a few districts near the river, except for a couple of high-class brothels that were secreted on Royal and Chartres Streets in the French Quarter.

Vice began to boom in the late 1840s, as New Orleans came into its own as a major city. During this period, the city's government was notoriously corrupt, and this allowed prostitution to begin to leave the recognized underworld sections and establish itself in the new quarter above Canal Street, especially that section lying north and northwest of St. Charles Avenue. Aside from a few futile gestures from reform groups, nothing was done to attempt to curb the spread of vice into this area. The politicians were useless, having already been bribed into submission, and they had no interest in the ruinous effects on the real estate in the neighborhood or the complaints of hundreds of property owners who were forced by the proximity of the bawdy houses to abandon their homes. The movement was encouraged rather than hampered by the Union soldiers during the Civil War and by the carpetbaggers who brought the city to the verge of ruin during Reconstruction. It has been written that by 1870, more than 190,000 bordellos of every kind of viciousness, from the expensive parlor house to the fifteen-cent crib, were running wide open in New Orleans. There was scarcely a block in the city that did not contain at least one brothel.

For nearly five decades, starting in the mid-1800s, brothels operated with little or no concealment in New Orleans and paid tribute to local politicians, the police and various city and state governments. The payments were divided according to the size of the brothel and how much business was being carried out. During some occasions, like Mardi Gras, when the city was filled with free-spending strangers, graft payments would increase. During times of depression, quick-thinking politicians not only omitted their regular collections but frequently also advanced money to the brothels to pay their running expenses until business improved, when they shared heavily in the gross income.

The rank and file of the police department seldom shared in the larger tributes that went to their political superiors, so they imposed their own levies. From the inmate of a crib, they extorted about twenty-five cents a week and managed to get one dollar out of a prostitute in an elegant parlor house. Payments for officials and politicians were usually collected by trusted saloonkeepers or civilian agents, but the money for the policeman on the beat was usually left on the stoop on designated nights in little piles of quarters and dollars. Policemen often came into the station house on certain nights with their pockets bulging with coins.

Prostitution was not actually against the law in New Orleans, but a wide variety of laws sprang up to ensure that prostitution could be controlled— for a price, of course. In one early law, a prostitute could only be punished if she "shall occasion scandals or disturb the tranquility of the neighborhood." In 1837, a law was passed that empowered the mayor, upon receipt of a petition signed by three respectable citizens, to order the removal of prostitutes from any premises against which a complaint was made. In 1845, the number of petitioners required was reduced by two. In 1839, prostitutes were prohibited from occupying the ground floor of a building, and another law was passed that made it forbidden for them to frequent, or drink in, any coffeehouse or cabaret. Various other ordinances prohibited them from disturbing the peace, accosting men from open doorways or windows or living with white and black prostitutes in the same house. The laws were seldom ever enforced, but their creation made it necessary for the brothel-keepers and prostitutes to continue paying protection money to those who were supposed to be enforcing them.

THE BORDELLOS OF BASIN STREET

While there were other sections of New Orleans that gained sordid reputations as abodes of vice, none of them reached the notoriety of Basin Street, which began at St. Peter Street in the French Quarter and ran southward to Canal and in the same general direction through the American section to Toledano Street. Although long vanished from any map of New Orleans, the memory of Basin Street still lives on in stories, old photographs and blues songs.

For almost a half century, Basin Street was the main artery of the red-light district, running right through the heart of the city; and during a greater part of that time, after about 1880, it was entirely given over to vice from St. Louis Street to Tulane Avenue. Both sides of the street were lined with the most ostentatious, luxurious and expensive brothels in America. They were three-story mansions of brick and brownstone, filled with hand-carved mahogany woodwork, Oriental rugs, silver doorknobs, grand pianos, marble fireplaces, copies of famous paintings and statuary, lavish furnishings and all of the finest things that could be purchased or imported. Only wine and champagne were served in these places. The ladies wore evening gowns and, in many places, could not be seen without an appointment. When not entertaining in the luxurious bedrooms, the ladies escorted their gentleman callers into rooms where musicians, dancers and singers performed nightly.

A few of the larger brothels were staffed by as many as thirty women, each of whom paid her madam from thirty to fifty dollars a week for food and lodging and more for laundry and other incidentals. The fees paid by the customers ranged from five to twenty dollars for a single experience and from

Basin Street in 1903. *Courtesy of the New Orleans Public Library.*

twenty to fifty dollars if he wished to spend the entire night. This included breakfast in the morning and, if needed, cab fare home. In later years, as Basin Street declined considerably in tone, the rates saw a drastic reduction. During this period, plenty of women on Basin Street were available for as little as one dollar. The wine changed to beer, the evening gowns to plain frocks or nothing at all, the performers to erotic exhibitions and the string quartets to tin whistles or a piano. It was a drastic change but not much different than the one that changed Basin Street from a quiet residential neighborhood to one of the most controversial thoroughfares in the city.

Basin Street's evolution began in the 1830s, when New Orleans began experiencing its first real significant growth in population. The street became one of the finest residential districts in the city, with handsome shade trees and imposing mansions occupied by wealthy American families. But it was not to last. By the end of the Civil War, Basin Street had begun to change. Unfortunately, it lay directly in the path of the prostitutes as they began moving north and east away from the earlier underworld areas, where brothels had been established before the war. A few sporting houses were apparently located on Basin Street as early as 1860, but the first of the large bordellos was established by Kate Townsend in 1866. According to rumor, the house was built at the joint expense of a police department official, a recorder and several members of the City Council. The names of the men were never made public, which made it merely sordid New Orleans gossip, but it was likely true. Kate Townsend was one of the most influential

Many of the brothels of Basin Street were regarded as the finest in the country. Marguerite Griffin was one of the prime attractions at Minnie White's sporting house. Not only was she popular with the men, but she also knew the lyrics to countless bawdy ballads. *Photograph by Ernest Bellocq.*

courtesans in the history of the city, and for many years, especially during the time the northern carpetbaggers were in power, her bordello was a favorite meeting place for politicians and city officials.

Her successful move to Basin Street paved the way for such an influx of prostitutes that within a few years, the finest part of the neighborhood above Canal Street had lost all semblance of respectability. Some of the harlots and madams who followed Kate onto Basin Street remained there for many years, and their names and establishments have become some of the most enduring legends of the city.

A dark-skinned beauty who called herself Minnie Haha, and claimed to be a descendant of the heroine in Longfellow's poem, opened a swanky brothel on Basin Street near the Townsend mansion in 1868. At the curb in front of her house, she installed a huge granite hitching post equipped with gilded iron rings. Her name was chiseled into it in large letters, and it was attended by a uniformed black boy—he wore a scarlet jacket with "Minnie Haha, Welcome" embroidered on it in gold—to take gentlemen's carriages. For the horses, Minnie provided a bag of apples, and when a man spent the night at the house, he awoke to find his clothing pressed and his shoes shined. Minnie prided herself on running a full-service establishment.

A few doors down, Leila Barton opened a fashionable sporting house in 1870. It was the scene of a small scandal in March of that year when the wife of a "well-known merchant" broke into the house and fired a pistol at Blanche Russell, an inmate of the house whom the wife believed was her husband's mistress. Only one bullet was fired, which went wild, and then the gun misfired. No one was hurt in the incident.

Another house was opened nearby by Gentle Annie Reed, but about 1870, she moved out and the house was taken over by Kitty Johnson, a madam known for her string of lovers. Two of them, Billy Walsh and J.J. Heley, fought a duel on the sidewalk in front of the bordello in 1882, while Kitty and her girls watched from the window. The winner of the duel had been promised a full-course dinner, prepared by Kitty's cook, who had won fame for the establishment based on its fine meals. After several shots were exchanged, Walsh was mortally wounded. Newspaper accounts do not state whether Heley enjoyed his meal before being taken away by the police.

On the opposite side of Basin Street was a brothel that belonged to Josephine Killen. In 1870, the big attraction at the place was the ten-year-old daughter of Mollie Williams, an inmate of the resort. The mother and child were sold jointly for fifty dollars a night. When the police felt this was going too far and took the child away, Josephine Killen denounced their actions, stating that the child was just helping her mother to put food on the table.

Another Basin Street brothel was the Twenty-One (located at No. 21 Basin Street). It was opened in 1870 by Hattie Hamilton, who earned a place in notorious New Orleans history. Hattie grew up as Hattie Peacock and was the daughter of a prosperous merchant in Port Richmond, New York. She was married in New York on March 3, 1855. Her husband, Samuel W. Plume, took her to Cuba, where the couple had one son. The history of the Plume family becomes a little confused at this point, but it is known that her husband sent her back to New York when he learned that her name was on the roster of a Havana brothel. A few years later, he moved to New Orleans with his son.

In 1864, Hattie turned up in New Orleans in the company of a man who called himself Colonel Hamilton. For the next year or so, she was a familiar figure in the restaurants and theatres of the city, and Colonel Hamilton made quite a name for himself as a gambler. Meanwhile, her husband continued to work as a police officer and raise the couple's son. It is unknown if they had any contact with each other at that point.

During this time, Hattie was renowned in New Orleans for her beauty and charm, but she also began to acquire a reputation for promiscuity. Colonel Hamilton eventually tired of her, and in 1866, Samuel Plume officially filed for divorce after he learned she was in the city and had become an inmate of Tilly Phillips's brothel on Rampart Street. Early in 1869, she moved to Julia Davis's bordello on Customhouse Street, one of the worst dives in the city, and in April of that year, she was one of three harlots arrested for fighting. The arresting officer was, coincidentally, Samuel Plume.

A few months after this, when it seemed things couldn't get any worse, Hattie's luck began to change for the better. She met Senator James D. Beares when he came to visit the brothel one night. The legislator was so taken with her beauty that he took her out of the brothel, bought her a fine wardrobe and installed her as the madam of the elegant bordello at No. 21 Basin Street. With Hattie's expert management skills, and a collection of beautiful women on staff, it became one of the most popular sporting houses in the city. For a time, thanks to the influence of the senator, it seriously threatened Kate Townsend's resort as the most popular spot for local politicians.

Once No. 21 was well established, Hattie left the day-to-day operations in the hands of a housekeeper and began spending most of her time at the home of Senator Beares on St. Charles Avenue. She posed as his wife and indulged in all manner of vice, including prolonged drinking bouts that went on for days. On the night of May 26, 1870, Hattie and Beares began drinking heavily after dinner, and several times during the night, Beares's butler, Robert Phillips, heard them quarrelling and heard scuffling in the bedroom. After dawn, he heard what sounded like a gunshot and, a few minutes later, found Beares lying on the couch, dying from a bullet wound to the abdomen. Hattie was sitting in a chair next to him, very drunk, staring at the man as he bled. On the floor between them was a pistol—which subsequently disappeared and was never found.

Phillips didn't immediately call the police. He first summoned George Beares, the senator's brother, who then contacted the authorities. This was only the start of a series of incidents that newspapers called "irregular." None of it was ever adequately explained. Hattie was taken into custody following the belated arrival of the police, but she was not formally arrested. She was held for twenty-four hours and then released—without ever being questioned. George Beares stated that he did not believe Hattie was guilty of wrongdoing. Instead, he accused the Negro butler, Robert Phillips, who was arrested and charged as an accessory to murder. Then, on June 7, when brought before an inquest into the murder, George Beares said that he knew nothing about his brother's murder and refused to testify. At the inquest, Patrick Clark, a close friend of the senator and a frequent guest at the house, said that he had never seen Robert Phillips before he appeared in court. Consequently, it was decided that the butler didn't do it, and Phillips was released. After that, the investigation was abandoned. The general belief in New Orleans was that Hattie and Phillips knew far too many of the senator's secrets and that his friends and relatives decided that it was better to let them go than pursue the circumstances of the murder.

Business at No. 21 dropped off in the aftermath of the senator's murder, and a year or so later, Hattie sold the place and opened another brothel on Customhouse Street. It remained in business as a notorious sporting house for the next ten years. She died in Old Point Comfort, Virginia, on August 9, 1882, leaving all of her property to David Jackson, the owner of the Gem concert saloon on Royal Street. Jackson had looked after Hattie's affairs and managed the records for her brothel since 1877. The newspapers guessed that Hattie's estate was worth about $200,000.00, but in probate court it was revealed that she only had $2,149.75. After the debts were paid, $719.20 remained after a lifetime of vice.

Jackson, however, did not even receive this modest sum. John J. Plume, Hattie's long lost son, appeared and contested the will. The court ruled against Jackson, and Plume received the money left from Hattie's estate—hardly an amount that was worth living a lifetime without his mother.

THE MURDER OF KATE TOWNSEND

Kate Townsend was one of New Orleans's most notorious brothel-keepers, but little was known about her life. Most of what could be discovered was found out after her death, when newspaper reporters began searching for heirs to her considerable fortune. Two mysteries remained in her life once the muckraking was finished—why the initials "A. PIMM" were tattooed on her arm and what really happened in a locked bed chamber that led to her death.

Kate, whose real name was Katherine Cunningham, was born in Liverpool, England, in 1839. Her father was a dockworker and at age fifteen, she went to work as a barmaid in a dance house on Paradise Street in Liverpool. According to Kate, she remained a virgin until she was seventeen, the age she met Peter Kearnaghan, a handsome young sailor whose life she saved during an altercation in the dance house. To show his appreciation to her, Kearnaghan got her pregnant with twins and sailed out of her life. The twins were born while he was away, and when he returned to Liverpool, Kate gave him a beating and complained to the police. The young sailor ended up with a six-month stretch in jail. Not long after, Kate abandoned her children, changed her name and fled to America.

Kate ended up in New Orleans in 1857. She became an inmate of Clara Fisher's brothel and worked there for about six months. From there, she went to a row of two-story brick houses on Canal Street, between Basin and Rampart, and then to Maggie Thompson's place on Customhouse Street, the last place in which she was simply a prostitute.

In her later years, Kate Townsend became grossly overweight, and she weighed over three hundred pounds at the time of her death. According to one of the newspapers, "Kate was a very portly woman and attracted general attention on the street. As she grew in age, she became afflicted with what was properly a deformity, a voluminous bust which never failed to provoke astonishment in those who chanced to meet her." But when Kate came to New Orleans, she was said to have been a beautiful girl with a lush, full figure, making her the most popular employee of whatever house she worked at. This popularity allowed her to save a great amount of money, and in 1863, she was able to leave Maggie Thompson's place and open a place of her own. She prospered at the new house and began making friends and acquiring influence among politicians and city officials. With their assistance, she was able to build a three-story brownstone at No. 40 Basin Street, which became one of the city's most luxurious sporting houses.

Kate occupied a large suite of rooms on the first floor of the building and reportedly spent $40,000 decorating her home in great fashion. The rest of the house was furnished in gaudy magnificence, and every floor boasted an overabundance of gilt, plate glass, velvet and damask. The building and contents was said to have cost well over $200,000, and the manner in which the bordello was conducted, at least for the first several years, was in keeping with its lavish appointments. Only a high-class trade was encouraged, and lower persons who occasionally made it into the place were thrown out by Kate herself. The number of girls regularly on duty varied between ten and twenty. Each girl was given one day off each week, and all of them were schooled in the art of being a lady. Evening dress was required, and bawdy talk and lewd behavior were not allowed. When a gentleman arrived, he was met at the door by a uniformed maid. If he was a steady client, many of whom had charge accounts, he was ushered into the drawing room, where he was expected to buy wine for the assembled company. If the man was a stranger, he was shown into an anteroom and questioned by Kate, who also drank a glass of wine with him, which he paid for, of course. If his credentials were in order, he was ushered into the drawing room and allowed to pick from the girls. Once he made his choice, they discreetly retired to the young woman's boudoir for a price of usually $15. A few of the more popular girls earned $20. Kate Townsend herself was occasionally available for the entertainment of a particularly distinguished client at the going rate of $50 an hour.

The operation brought Kate great prosperity for the next half dozen years, but as the power of the politicians upon whom she depended began to wane, she was compelled to abandon some of her stricter rules, lower her rates and open the brothel to men of lesser wealth and importance. The new clients brought almost as much money into the house in the long run, but the fact that Kate had to lower her standards in such a way weighed so heavily on her mind that she began to display a mean streak and a violent temper, which naturally drove away some of the trade.

The house also suffered a serious, though temporary, setback in 1870 when Gus Taney, a young gambler who was known for the fact that he habitually carried a derringer, a revolver, a bowie-knife, a slung-shot and a hide-out knife on his person at all times, was murdered in the drawing room by Jim White, a fellow gambler. On July 30, Taney and White, both drunk, visited Kate's place. Taney ordered a $10.00 bottle of wine, but when he started to pay for it, he found that he only had $2.50 in his pockets. Kate told him that he could pay for it another time, but White made a disparaging comment about a man who couldn't pay for what he ordered. Taney accused White of stealing his money, and White lunged at him. Taney drew his revolver, but before he could use it, White stabbed him in the heart with a nine-inch blade. Taney's revolver was found on the floor by the police, who gave it and the knife to Kate to keep as souvenirs. After that, she slept with the knife under her pillow and carried it with her everywhere she went. It turned out to be the knife that she was murdered with.

Early on in her career, Kate met Treville "Bill" Egbert Sykes, a member of a good New Orleans family, and formed a relationship with him that lasted almost twenty-five years. In 1878, Sykes, down on his luck, moved into a second-floor room in Kate's brothel. In return for board and lodging, he was supposed to keep accounts and make himself useful around the place. He lived there for five years, during which time, according to his story, he led "a dog's life." Kate allegedly beat him, locked him in his room, refused to give him spending money, cut off one of his toes with her knife and frequently threatened to kill him when he refused her orders. Kate, on the other hand, often complained that Sykes was jealous and a thief and that he interfered with her business. A few months after he took up residence in her house, she had him arrested for forging her signature to five checks that totaled up to $7,000. She later refused to prosecute, and the charges were dropped.

Kate's troubles with Sykes reached a climax in October 1883, when she became infatuated with a young man named McLern, who often came to the house, borrowed money and allowed Kate to lavish him with gifts. Sykes protested and tried to throw McLern out of the house. He ended up being beaten by Kate and her new lover. On the day after the beating, Kate was in the kitchen with Molly Johnson when she picked up a butcher's knife and told the other woman that she had "half a mind to open Sykes' belly." Molly managed to dissuade her from this, and Kate compromised by summoning Sykes into the kitchen and beating him with a breadboard. A few hours later, Molly met her on the stairway. She was still brandishing the butcher's knife and threatening to kill Sykes if she could find him.

On the night of November 1, Kate and Molly met McLern and another man on Canal Street. The four of them got drunk in a local café, where Kate and McLern quarreled. McLern threatened her with a champagne bottle but apologized when Kate drew out her knife. "I've got to cut somebody," she was heard to say. "I'll go home and open Sykes' belly."

When they returned to Basin Street, Molly warned Sykes, who locked and barred his door. Kate never bothered him that night and, in fact, remained in her room until November 3, sleeping off a terrible hangover. At 9:30 that morning, though, Sykes went to Kate's room. The housekeeper, Mary Philomene, heard screams a short time later and found Sykes and Kate fighting in her bedroom. Sykes threw the maid out into the hall and locked the door. She heard more screams, thrashing, glass breaking and more commotion and then, after several minutes, Sykes opened the door. He was bleeding from cuts on his left breast and below his knee. His clothing was torn to shreds. "Well, Mary," he said to the maid, "she's gone."

The police were summoned, and word quickly spread that Kate Townsend had been murdered by her lover. The authorities found eleven wounds on Kate's body, three of them fatal. Sykes told the police that soon after he went into her room she drew her knife from under her pillow and attacked him. He managed to get the knife away from her and then she attacked him again, this time with a pair of scissors. He killed her, he swore, in self-defense.

Kate's body, dressed in a $600 white silk gown, was laid out in the drawing room, and at the funeral, champagne was served to all of the guests. She was buried in a $400 metal coffin that bore a silver cross that was inscribed with her name, her age and the date of her death. The body was followed to the cemetery by a procession of twenty carriages—there was not a man in any of them. The public administrator took charge of the brothel and soon afterward leased it to Molly Johnson, who operated it until her death in 1889. After that, the house was closed and the contents were auctioned off. The property later became an Elks lodge.

Bill Sykes was tried for Kate's murder but was acquitted. No one could prove that his claims of self-defense were not true, even though no one really knew what had occurred in the locked bedroom. Sykes produced a will, dated September 1873, in which Kate had bequeathed him her entire estate. It was admitted to probate, with Sykes as the executor, but he was removed in February 1884 for pocketing money that was supposed to go to the estate. At the same time, the state's attorney general asked the courts to reduce Sykes's claim to Kate's money to only 10 percent of the entire estate since he and Kate had lived together but had never been married, a law that was enforced at the time. Sykes fought the judgment against him in every court in Louisiana but eventually lost. Kate's estate was finally settled in 1888, and by the time the state managed to steal everything it could from it, the account amounted to $33,142.65. The lawyers got about $30,000 of it, and most of the rest went to court costs and other expenses. In the end, Sykes—Kate's killer—ended up with $34.

LOOSE LADIES OF NEW ORLEANS

During the period that saw the rise and fall of Hattie Hamilton and Kate Townsend, there were many other brothels operating in the city that were quite different from the luxurious mansions of Basin Street. Many low cribs and cheap parlor houses could be found on Dauphine, Burgundy, St. Louis, Conti, Customhouse and Bienville Streets in the French Quarter and on Franklin Street and the upper end of Gasquet Street in the American section. The worst dive on Gasquet Street was a crib house known as Pig-Trough Carrie's, which opened about 1870; while on Franklin Street were such notorious spots as the Picayune House and McCarty's Ranch, a combination brothel, dance hall and gambling den.

During the same period that saw the luxurious brothels on Basin Street, a number of cribs and dives were also operating in New Orleans. These dirty and dangerous places offered prostitutes for as little as fifteen cents.

In the Dauphine and Burgundy Street vice areas, women both white and black worked together indiscriminately and were patronized by men of all races and colors, a situation that persisted both before the Civil War and after, making this one of the first desegregated places in the state. From about 1850 to the early 1880s, except for a few cleanup efforts, conditions in this area were unbelievably bad. Virtually every building on the street was a brothel, filled with fighting, diseased harlots of the lowest kind. The whole area swarmed with streetwalkers and pimps, and in the absence of more permanent quarters, prostitutes flung down an old piece of carpet on the sidewalk and entertained their clients in full view of passersby and the workers in the houses, who screamed out advice and abuse and kept pails of water handy to discourage the use of doorsteps. Inside the brothels, prices ranged from fifteen to fifty cents. On the sidewalk, the standing rate was a dime.

At No. 111 Dauphine Street was a brothel that was described by newspapers in 1885 as the worst Negro dive in the city. In earlier days, though, it had been occupied by white prostitutes and gained considerable renown because of the tragic end of one of its inmates, Nellie Gaspar. Nellie, the daughter of a London innkeeper, came to New Orleans in 1866 as a performer in Smith's European Circus. She was seduced by a local pimp who forced her into working at the Dauphine Street brothel. She later died after being beaten by her "lover." Nellie was found in her room by the brothel-keeper, an ugly harridan called Madame Schneider, who locked her in and traded water for the girl's dresses until her wardrobe ran out. Nellie was then taken to Charity Hospital but discharged three days later. She returned to the brothel on Dauphine Street but died a week later.

On Burgundy Street, between Bienville and Conti, was "Smoky Row," a half dozen or so dilapidated old houses that were the worst that New Orleans had to offer. The dives were filled with black prostitutes of all ages, from ten to seventy, who, when not fighting or otherwise occupied, sat on rickety chairs in doorways, smoking and chewing tobacco. When a man passed, they tried to drag him inside. If they managed to get him into the dark interiors of the house, he could count on being beaten and robbed. Smoky Row remained a blight on the city until 1885, when so many complaints about it were made to the police that they had to do something about it. In July, the residents were evicted and the houses torn down. Police officers found piles of bloodstained wallets and men's clothing in the ruins, which launched a search of the courtyard for bodies. Nothing was ever found, but many officers believed that corpses were hidden somewhere on the grounds.

THE BRIGHT LIGHTS OF STORYVILLE

By the 1890s, the authorities of New Orleans finally came to the realization that unless some sort of suppressive or regulatory measures were carried out, the city would eventually be transformed into one large vice district. Several regulatory ordinances were proposed but failed, including one that provided for a segregated vice district and the issuing of licenses to prostitutes. The measure fell before the united opposition of clergymen and women's groups, which advanced the argument that such a law would recognize the existence of vice in New Orleans—which, at this point, was very hard to miss.

Nothing further was done about the matter until January 26, 1897, when the City Council adopted the now famous ordinance introduced by Alderman Sidney Story that would set aside an area where prostitution would be not only permitted but actually legal. The ordinance was changed and adapted several times before it was finally determined that this red-light

After making a study of red-light districts in European cities, New Orleans alderman Sidney Story proposed a segregated vice district for the city. Once it was organized, it was called "Storyville" in his honor—much to the timid alderman's chagrin.

district would comprise a five-block area on each of Customhouse, Bienville, Conti and St. Louis Streets and three each on North Basin, Treme, Villere, Marais, North Franklin and North Robertson Streets—a total of thirty-eight blocks occupied solely by brothels, saloons, cabarets and other enterprises that depended on vice for their prosperity.

The removal of prostitutes to these streets, several of which were already well filled with bordellos, began during the late summer of 1897 and was in full swing on October 1, when the Story ordinance went into effect. By the middle of 1898, the movement had been completed, and the new district, popularly known as "Storyville"—much to the alderman's chagrin—began operating under the law. The brothels were now safe from interference by the police so long as they conducted themselves with restraint and no crimes were committed in them.

Within a few years, Storyville became the most celebrated red-light district in the United States, and tourists came from all over to both see and experience it. The gateway to Storyville was the property of Thomas C. Anderson, saloonkeeper, political boss of the Fourth Ward, member of the legislature for two terms, owner of at least one of the most prosperous sporting houses in the district and the unofficial "mayor" of Storyville.

Anderson owned a restaurant and cabaret on Rampart Street, as well as several other places. His main establishment, the Annex, was the most important place in the district and served as the "town hall."

Anderson's right-hand man in the operation of his various enterprises was Billy Struve, a young crime reporter who first met Anderson about 1895. Struve helped him organize the Astoria Club, one of his first important ventures. He began working for Anderson full time in 1900, abandoning his newspaper work. In 1907, Anderson gave him a piece of his business, and the two remained close friends until the end of Anderson's life. With Struve's help, Storyville's "mayor" amassed a great fortune and retained his political power and prestige until the district was eventually closed down. About the time of Prohibition, Anderson retired from the saloon business and invested his wealth in oil. He organized the Protection Oil Company, which later became Liberty Oil and was later bought out by Standard Oil. In 1928, Anderson became very ill and feared that he was going to die. He recovered, though, and afterward became a religious man. In September, he

This saloon belonged to Tom Anderson, the unofficial "mayor" of Storyville. He was the political boss of the Fourth Ward, and Storyville boomed during his years in power. Farther up the street in this photograph is the lavish brothel (building with the cupola) that belonged to Josie Arlington, Storyville's most famous madam. *Courtesy of the New Orleans Public Library.*

married Gertrude Hoffmire, who was known as Gertrude Dix when she was operating two brothels, owned by Anderson, on Basin Street. Anderson died in December 1931 and left his entire estate to his widow.

Storyville boomed during Anderson's years as the district's leader. As in the days of Kate Townsend, the area along North Basin Street remained the site of the new district's swankiest brothels. The imposing three- and four-story mansions were bordellos where business was conducted with considerable elegance and ceremony. Rudeness and lewd behavior on the part of the customers was frowned upon, and drunken gentlemen were not accommodated. When a man entered the parlor, he was expected to buy a drink—incidentally, at great profit to the house—but the girls were not brought out for inspection unless he requested it. All of the sporting houses were more or less expensively furnished and equipped, with as much gilt and velvet as the madams and their financial backers could afford. Many of them had one or more rooms with mirrored walls and ceilings, which were available at special rates; ballrooms with hardwood floors for dancing; and curtained stages for indecent performances and erotic displays that were given whenever sufficient money was offered.

A few of the best places employed orchestras that performed in the ballroom of the house from evening until closing time, which was usually at dawn. Others depended on the groups of itinerant musicians who frequently appeared in Storyville, playing in the streets and saloons for coins and drinks.

Jazz music, contrary to the beliefs of some, was not born in Storyville. It was already around by the time that the district came into being. Jazz, which was different than blues and ragtime, first appeared as music to be played joyfully in the open air by the brass bands of New Orleans's countless fraternal organizations at the parades, picnics and events that have long been a part of the city's social life. Many people, however, considered jazz "whorehouse music," perhaps because Storyville gave employment to scores of jazz musicians in the early 1900s. These groundbreaking musicians soon reached a new audience, including reporters who were writing stories about the bordellos, thus connecting jazz and vice for their readers. Whether the connection was deserved or not, Storyville began the careers of many musicians who went on to great fame like Jelly Roll Morton, Joseph "King" Oliver, Tony Jackson, Clarence Williams, Manuel Manetta, Oscar "Papa" Celestin, Frank "Dude" Amacker, Steve Lewis and many others. The musicians who played in the brothels, many becoming an attraction on their own, were referred to as "professors," a term of respect for their musical abilities.

Storyville jazz legend Tony Jackson.

The famous Jelly Roll Morton was another jazz musician who got his start in Storyville.

During the two decades of the district's existence, perhaps two hundred or so fine jazz musicians worked the mansions of Storyville. Little record of them remains today but their occasionally repeated names and a whispered legend of a time when music rolled out of bordello windows and echoed down Basin Street.

But not all of the artists who came to Storyville were musicians. One of them was a little man who walked like a duck, had a high, squeaky voice and was a grotesque hydrocephalic (water on the brain) with more beauty to offer the world than just about anyone else of his era. His name was Ernest J. Bellocq, a New Orleans photographer who worked from about 1895 through the late 1930s. He was active in Storyville during the 1910s, and thanks to his good relationships with the various madams, he became the "official" photographer of the district. Only a few of his Storyville pictures survived—eighty-nine glass plates, many of which were broken or damaged—and they were found in his desk after his death. Most of them are portraits of prostitutes, and many of them are nudes. After Bellocq's death, many of the plates were defaced, allegedly by his brother, a Catholic priest, who wanted to conceal the identities of the subjects.

Dozens, perhaps hundreds, of photographers came to Storyville during its existence, just as they did to the red-light districts of Chicago, San Francisco and other cities, in search of uninhibited models. There was good money to be made in "French postcards." Bellocq was different, though. There is no evidence that he ever took a pornographic picture. His photographs exhibited sensitivity and a feeling for his subjects. The women were not treated as objects, and that elevated his photographs to the level of art. He was apparently accepted by the women of Storyville, perhaps because he was like them. His medical problems essentially isolated him from polite society, and like the women, he was an object of society's contempt. No one can say just what connection was felt between Bellocq and the women of Storyville, but there is no denying that a rapport existed between them. In his eyes, and through the lens of his camera, these women were transformed into something that was beyond their everyday life.

CHRONICLES OF STORYVILLE

The happenings of the harlots of New Orleans were faithfully chronicled for almost thirty years in a half-dozen different publications, each with their own brand of notoriety. The best known and most influential were the

The *Mascot* made for lurid reading and offered the first advertisements for prostitutes in New Orleans.

Mascot, Sunday Sun and the *Blue Book*. The *Mascot* was established in 1882 and was put out every Saturday for five cents a copy. It was four to six pages long and published sensational accounts of crime and scandal. During the early 1890s, the *Mascot* began to devote considerable space to the activities of the red-light district and, in 1894, started a column called simply "Society," in which were published personal items about the prostitutes. None of them was lewd or lascivious. The items spoke of new girls who had arrived in various houses and items of gossip about the women and their customers.

These news items and comments were the models of propriety when compared with those published in the *Sunday Sun*, which first appeared in 1888 and was always a full-blown scandal sheet. It appeared on newsstands and at local saloons, also selling for five cents, every Saturday. The front page was almost invariably devoted to a murder, divorce case or some other scandal. However, the feature that accounted for the considerable success of the paper was a column called "Scarlet World," which was filled with frank comments about the doings of the local prostitutes.

The *Blue Book*, the most famous of New Orleans's red-light publications, was the last of a series of directories of the district. The first of these was the *Green Book, or A Gentleman's Guide to New Orleans*. It was published in January 1895 in an edition of two thousand copies, which quickly sold out. A few years later, the *Red Book* appeared and was just as successful. The first issue of the *Blue Book*, financed by Tom Anderson and edited by former newspaper writer Billy Struve, was published in 1902, and it appeared every year for a number of years afterward. Each edition was forty to fifty pages long and sold for a quarter a copy in the local saloons; it was also peddled by agents

The *Blue Book* was the official guide to the prostitutes and sporting houses of Storyville and featured advertising not only from the various bordellos but also from taverns, restaurants, tobacco shops and other places that would be of interest to men.

at the hotels, the railroad stations and the steamboat landings. It was bound in blue paper, and the cover was decorated with flowers and the words "Blue Book," all printed with red ink.

The book contained a preface and a warning that "this book must not be mailed," which prevented readers from sending illegal material through the mail. The book contained a complete list of all the prostitutes in residence in Storyville, both black and white, arranged by location in some issues and alphabetically in others. At the top of each page of names was a decorative drawing of two women facing each other with a red light between them. In the front and middle portions of the book were advertisements for saloons, lawyers, restaurants, cabarets, breweries, cigars and tobacco. The last fifteen or twenty pages were devoted to announcements by the brothel owners, with the names of the madams and the street addresses in red.

The *Blue Book* went through five editions, with the final edition appearing in 1912. It was reprinted in 1915. The last edition was over two hundred pages long and was the most sophisticated of Struve's promotional efforts. The directly listed a total of 773 prostitutes.

Many years later, the *Blue Book* remains a fascinating and unique document of the life and times of Storyville.

JOSIE ARLINGTON

Despite the extravagant claims made in the *Blue Book* and in assorted advertising of the times, none of the lavish brothels in Storyville could match the extravagance of the Arlington, which was operated at No. 225 North Basin Street by Josie Arlington, the most celebrated madam of her time. She was to Storyville what Kate Townsend had been to the red-light district of the earlier time.

Josie Arlington's house was the most popular brothel in Storyville. It was a towering, four-story mansion with bay windows on three sides and a cupola on the roof. It was modestly painted on the outside, but the interior was filled with gilt, velvet hangings, Oriental rugs, damask couches and chairs, lace curtains, beveled mirrors, glass chandeliers and rooms jammed in the crowded style of the Victorian era. Few of the many rival establishments offered more than a half dozen girls, but the Arlington always had at least ten waiting in the parlor. During tourist and Mardi Gras seasons, that number doubled. The girls were always the most exquisite ones in the district, too. They were always clad in expensive—and revealing—French lingerie and entertained

The Vienna Parlor at Josie Arlington's bordello in Storyville.

The American Parlor at Josie Arlington's bordello in Storyville.

the cream of New Orleans society. Many of the men who came to Josie's were politicians, judges, lawyers, bankers, doctors and even city officials.

Josie's real name was Mary Deubler. She was born in New Orleans about 1864 and was never married. In 1881, she fell in love with a gambler and pimp named Philip Lobrano, and she was his mistress for nine years. During that time, she was an inmate of various brothels in the city, using the name Josie Alton.

About 1888, Josie began using the name Lobrano and opened a place of her own on Customhouse Street. It soon became known as one of the toughest houses in New Orleans, but Josie still made enough money to support several members of her family and Lobrano, who lived in the house with her. Lobrano hated her relatives, and on November 2, 1890, during a terrible fight in which Josie and all of her girls were involved, Lobrano shot her brother, Peter Deubler. Lobrano was tried twice, and at the second trial, he was acquitted.

After the shooting, Josie broke with her lover and changed her name to Lobrano d'Arlington. She dismissed the low women who worked for her and announced that she planned to fill her house with gracious, tasteful girls who would appeal to gentlemen of refinement. She operated her newly renovated bordello on Customhouse Street until Storyville was established. Soon after, she opened the Arlington. It wasn't long before she acquired her upper-class reputation and became renowned for one of the grandest and gaudiest houses in America. Josie ran the place for ten years and amassed a considerable fortune. The only thing that Josie still craved was social acceptance, which was something she could never have. She was shunned by the families of the city and even publicly ignored by the men she knew so well. Her money and charm meant nothing to the society circles of New Orleans.

However, an incident occurred in 1905 that convinced her that what she could not have in life, she would have in death. After a fire badly damaged the interior of the Arlington and Josie barely escaped from the place with her life, she decided that she would prepare for her eventual death and, in so doing, would have her revenge on those who snubbed her. She purchased a plot of land in Metarie, the city's most fashionable cemetery, and erected a costly red marble tomb topped by two pillars. On the steps was placed a bronze statue of a woman who ascended the staircase with a bouquet of roses in the crook of her arm. The tomb was an amazing piece of funerary art, designed by an eminent architect named Albert Weiblen, and although it cost Josie a small fortune, it was worth every penny to her because of the

This photograph was taken during a dinner party that Josie Arlington (seated in front, to the left) gave in her home to celebrate the engagement of John T. Brady and Anna Deubler, Josie's niece. Several of the most prominent people in the city attended, including Mayor Martin Behrman. However, even the most lavish parties could not win her the social acceptance that she wanted. *Courtesy of the New Orleans Public Library*.

scandal it created. Tongues wagged all over the city, and the gossip only increased after Josie died in 1914.

A few months after her death, the city installed a red traffic light on the road alongside the cemetery. At night, the glow of the light struck the marble tomb in such a way that it gave the perfect illusion of a red light shining at the door of the brothel-keeper's tomb. The word quickly spread, and people came in droves to witness the bizarre sight. The cemetery was overrun with people every evening, which shocked the cemetery caretakers and the families of those buried on the grounds.

Scandal followed Josie even to her death.

THE END OF STORYVILLE

Vice in New Orleans was doomed by America's entrance into World War I. Early in August 1917, Secretary of War Newton D. Baker issued an order forbidding open prostitution within five miles of an army camp. A similar rule was made for naval bases, and later that same month, Bascom Johnson, representing the War and Navy Departments, visited New Orleans, inspected Storyville and informed Mayor Martin Behrman that it had to be closed down. Mayor Behrman protested all the way to Washington, but it was no use. If the city didn't close down Storyville, the military would do it for them.

An ordinance was adopted on October 9 and stated that after midnight on November 12, 1917, it would be illegal to operate a brothel anywhere in New Orleans. On Saturday night, November 10, two days before the new law went into effect, a large force of police officers was sent to Storyville to prevent the trouble that was expected to come from the closing. None developed, and in fact, the district was quieter than usual, as if in mourning. There were a few people in the streets, but most of the saloons, cabarets and brothels were empty. Many of them had already closed, and the red lights had been removed from the windows of others.

On November 11, Gertrude Dix appealed to the civil courts for an injunction that would prevent the city from closing the district, but the request was refused. The exodus from Storyville had actually started two weeks earlier, but most of the prostitutes had waited for the result of Gertrude Dix's application for a restraining order. When the news of her failure spread, wagons and vans began hauling away whatever furniture remained that had not been sold to the secondhand dealers. As late as midnight on November 12, there was still a parade of harlots, laden with property, leaving the district. The next afternoon, police officers visited every house and informed the women that if they remained in Storyville, they had to take down their red lights and they would be watched and arrested if they continued to operate. Gertrude Dix was one of the few who remained. After a few months, she reopened her house and ran it secretly until she was arrested by agents from the Department of Justice on May 13, 1918. Four other places were also raided. Gertrude entered a guilty plea and spent five days in the House of Detention.

On November 14, the *New Orleans Item* announced that the police planned to round up any of the men who came looking for prostitutes in what was once Storyville and send them out into the countryside to help the farmers. Needless to say, nothing came of this idea. The next day, many leading churchwomen and members of the Louisiana Federation of Women's Clubs held a meeting and put together a committee to help the prostitutes who had been driven out. No one ever applied for the promised aid. Few of the women of Storyville needed it. They had simply moved on to new locations in various business and residential sections of New Orleans and continued plying their profession.

THE MAFIA IN NEW ORLEANS

One of the most notorious crimes in New Orleans history was the 1890 assassination of David C.M. Hennessey, the first superintendent of the New Orleans Police Department. Accused of the crime were nineteen members of a Sicilian gang, and although acquitted of any wrongdoing, eleven of them were later lynched by a mob.

New Orleans at that time was probably the most anti-Italian city in America. The city had been flooded with thousands of Italian immigrants, and statements from the mayor's office didn't help matters any. In one letter, Mayor Joseph A. Shakespeare called Southern Italians and Sicilians "the most idle, vicious and worthless people among us."

Of course, not all of the blame for the bad feelings could be placed on the city government. New Orleans of the late 1800s was filled with corrupt politicians and police officers, but it was also overflowing with Italian criminals. There is no denying that the ghetto of the French Quarter was turning out productive Italian citizens, but it was also turning out criminals. Undoubtedly, many of these criminals were not "Mafiosi," but it has long been conceded that New Orleans represented one of the main ports of entry for the Mafia into the United States—a fact that would have a bloody effect on the history of the city.

Hennessey became the superintendent of the force during the administration of Mayor Joseph Shakespeare, who had won election as a reform candidate. One of the things that he promised to do during the election was to clean

Newly arrived Italian immigrants step off the boat at the New Orleans immigration station. The city's mayor, Joseph Shakespeare, called the Italians "the most idle, vicious and worthless people among us." By the late 1800s, New Orleans was the most anti-Italian city in America. *Courtesy of the Library of Congress.*

up the city's corrupt police department, and he made drastic plans to reorganize everything, get rid of the problem officers, increase the pay of the patrolmen and lay the groundwork for an efficient police force, which the city had never really had. One of his first acts after the election in April 1888 was appointing Hennessey as his chief of police.

Hennessey was born on March 4, 1857, the son of a policeman who was murdered in 1869 in a St. Ann Street coffeehouse. A year after his father's death, Hennessey became a messenger boy in the office of General A.S. Badger, who was then chief of police. After a few years, he worked his way up to an appointment in the detective bureau. He was teamed up with his cousin, Mike Hennessey, a former cab driver who had been appointed special policeman by Governor Nichols in 1877 and then detective two years later. A bitter feud had developed, the cause of which was unknown, between Mike Hennessey and the chief of aids, Thomas Devereaux, and the two men frequently exchanged threats. On October 31, 1881, the two Hennesseys met

Slain New Orleans police chief
David Hennessey.

Devereaux on Gravier Street, and the latter drew a revolver and fired. Mike fell to the street, and Devereaux advanced to shoot again, but both Mike and David fired first. Devereaux was killed. The Hennesseys were tried and acquitted on a plea of self-defense but were both kicked off the police force. Mike operated a detective agency in Galveston for a year and then moved to Houston, where he was murdered in September 1886 by an assassin who was said to have come from New Orleans expressly to kill him. David joined M.J. Farrell's Harbor Protection Police, a private agency, and was superintendent of the agency until his appointment by Mayor Shakespeare.

But almost from the day he took the oath of office as chief of police, he was marked for death by the Mafia, a notorious Sicilian crime organization.

No one really knows when the Mafia began to operate in America, but crime experts believe that it was in New Orleans in the late 1800s. Between 1888 and 1890, the New Orleans Mafia, made up of several Sicilian groups, committed dozens of murders without opposition.

During the time when the Mafia was gaining a foothold in New Orleans, one of the principal organized crime lieutenants in Sicily was Giuseppe Esposito, a small, notoriously fierce man with a heavy black beard and mustache. After the botched kidnapping of a British clergyman, soldiers killed a number of Mafia members in Sicily, but Esposito and several others escaped to the United States. After several weeks in New York, he came to New Orleans in March 1881 and rented a house on Chartres Street. At the time, the local Mafia was being run by Tony Labruzzo, who was shoved aside by Esposito when the new arrival began directing operations. Labruzzo resented the man's assumption of command, so he informed the Italian consul that the escaped Sicilian bandit was in New Orleans. The consul contacted the police and asked that Esposito be kept under surveillance until they received instructions from Italy. For the next several weeks, Esposito was shadowed day and night by Mike and David Hennessey.

Meanwhile, James Mooney and D. Boland, private detectives from New York, were searching for Esposito for the Italian government and traced him to New Orleans. They arrived in the city in July 1881 and, at a conference with Chief of Police Boylan, decided to arrest Esposito. On July 5, the Hennesseys captured the Sicilian in Jackson Square, rushed him into a carriage that Mooney and Boland had waiting and took him to the police station. He was soon spirited out of the city by the two New York detectives and sent back to Italy, where he began serving a life sentence in prison.

Ten days after Esposito's arrest, Tony Labruzzo was shot to death on Bienville Street. The Hennesseys received death threats of their own, but although Mike was killed in Houston five years later—allegedly by a Mafia gunman—it was ten years before the threats of violence against David Hennessey were carried out.

Soon after the capture of Esposito and the murder of Labruzzo, the Mafia in New Orleans came under the domination of a faction headed by Charles Matranga and his brother, Tony. Under their leadership, the Mafia began to expand. For several years, the Provenzano brothers— George, Joe and Peter—controlled the docks where ships from Central and South America unloaded their goods. They held contracts with the shipping companies and employed several hundred Italian workers at good wages. The Provenzanos were rich and politically influential and, so far as was ever known, had no connection to organized crime. In fact, they regularly paid tribute to the Matrangas and employed the men whom the mob bosses sent to them for work.

During the mid-1880s, the Matrangas began to challenge the Provenzano operations, informing the shipping companies that they would be unloading the vessels from now on and telling the Provenzanos to leave the docks. This was emphasized by attacks on the Provenzano men, during which several workers were shot. Unable to fight back against the mob, the Provenzanos abandoned their business, and the Matrangas took control of the docks.

They made enormous profits by immediately cutting the workers' wages and forcing the men, under threat of death, to accept the miserable pay. The Provenzanos opened a grocery store, but Matrangas destroyed their stock and intimidated their customers, causing this venture to fail. In desperation, the Provenzanos hired gunmen, and a war began that claimed about a dozen lives. The last encounter occurred in April 1888, when Tony Matranga and two of his men were ambushed at Claiborne Avenue and Esplanade Street. Joe and Peter Provenzano, along with three of their men, were arrested. After many delays, a trial date was set for October 17, 1890. The Matrangas employed some of the best lawyers in New Orleans to assist the prosecution.

Shortly after the ambush, David Hennessey became the chief of police. He had been friends with George and Peter Provenzano for many years and believed the men were on the right side in the battle with the Matrangas. He was aware of the fact that the murders among the city's Italians would not end until the power of the Mafia was destroyed. He began to collect evidence against the Matrangas and was soon warned about continuing his investigation. He ignored the death threats and announced publicly that he planned to present the evidence that he was collecting at the trial of the Provenzanos.

On the night of October 15, 1890, two days before he was to appear on the witness stand, Hennessey left his office and started for his home on Girod Street, between Basin and Franklin. He was accompanied by Captain William J. O'Connor of the Boylan Protective Police, who left Hennessey at Rampart and Girod Streets. O'Connor had walked less than half a block when he heard the sound of a shotgun blast, followed by three or four shots from a revolver. He hurried back and found Hennessey sitting on the stoop of a house. He was bleeding badly from four wounds on the left side of his body. Hennessy was gasping in pain and told his friend that he'd been shot but that he had given it back to his attackers as best he could. O'Connor asked him who had fired the shots. "Dagoes!" Hennessey whispered and then collapsed. He was rushed to Charity Hospital, where he died the next morning.

The murder of Chief Hennessey caused a furor in New Orleans. The funeral was held in the council chamber at city hall and was attended by the most prominent men in the state. The streets were lined with thousands of people as the procession made its way to the cemetery. For days after, the city buzzed with talk of lynching, and many Italians published notices in the newspapers disavowing any connection to the Mafia or to the suspects that were being rounded up by the police. Twenty-one Italians were arrested in connection with Hennessey's murder, nineteen of whom were indicted by a grand jury in November, eleven as principals and eight as accessories to the crime. On February 17, 1891, nine of the accused were brought to trial. The case went to the jury on March 12, and the verdict was returned the next day. Despite the conclusive nature of the evidence against them, the jury was unable to agree on three of the defendants and acquitted the others.

Almost immediately, proof emerged that the trial had been tampered with. Not only were many of the witnesses threatened and paid off, but members of the jury also reported being approached with bribes. The jury members who stayed silent had probably accepted the mob's money. It became increasingly clear that a detective who had been hired by the Matrangas, Dominick O'Malley, had won the case using Mafia money. An investigation was started by the grand jury and resulted in the indictment of O'Malley and a half dozen of his agents, several of whom were later convicted.

New Orleans's Italian immigrants were thrilled with the news of the verdicts. Many stands in the French Market, owned by Sicilians, were decorated with bunting and streamers. In the Parish Prison, the acquitted men, though still being held under an indictment for conspiracy, toasted one another and their lawyers with wine sent by their friends. Reports were spread of Sicilians who claimed that the Mafia was now running the city and there was nothing the police could do and of an American flag being torn down, trampled in the mud and then hoisted upside down beneath a banner of Italy. Many of the state's witnesses, who had received death threats from the Mafia, left the city or barricaded themselves in their homes after stocking up on food, guns and ammunition.

But while all of this was taking place, a meeting was being held at a Carondelet Street club that resulted in a notice that appeared in the morning newspaper. It called for a mass meeting on Canal Street at the junction of Royal and St. Charles. At the time, a statue of Henry Clay stood at this spot, and it was a popular common meeting ground. The rally had been called for by a large number of New Orleans's most prominent citizens to discuss the failure of justice in the Hennessey case. Those attending were advised to be prepared for action.

The crowd began arriving long before the appointed meeting time. Three of the organizers—William S. Parkerson, John C. Wickliffe and Walter Denegre—addressed the gathered attendees, reviewing the Hennessey case and denouncing the failure of the law to dispense justice. Since the courts refused to act, they said, the people of New Orleans would see that justice

The lynch mob gathered at the statue of Henry Clay that stood for many years at the busy intersection of Canal, St. Charles and Royal Streets. After roaring their approval to the men who planned the executions, the mob stormed the Parish Prison. Harper's Weekly, *March 28, 1891.*

was carried out. They told the crowd what they intended to do, asked for a sign of approval and received it in a great roar of applause. The last speaker, Wickliffe, announced that he and the two other men would head the execution party. As he stepped down from the statue's pedestal, the crowd began streaming down the street in the direction of the Parish Prison. The organizers of the rally formed ranks and marched into a Canal Street gun store, where they armed themselves with rifles and shotguns. From there, they went straight to the prison.

Word spread that a lynch mob was coming, and Sheriff Gabriel Villere left Captain Lemuel Davis in charge of the prison while he went to seek help from the military or the police. But no help was coming. Captain Davis locked all of the prisoners in their cells, except for the Italians, who were told to find hiding places wherever they could. When the mob arrived, they began clamoring at the locked doors of the prison, threatening to

An illustration of the lynch mob storming into the prison and shooting the men believed to have been involved in the Hennessey assassination. Harper's Weekly, *March 28, 1891.*

dynamite the building. Captain Davis refused to admit them, so Parkerson sent a small group of men around to Marais Street, where they broke open a seldom-used wooden door. A group of the men rushed inside, searching for the Hennessey murder suspects. Each of the men had a list of the eleven suspects in hand. These were the men believed to be guilty. The mob had strict instructions not to harm anyone else.

The unlucky eleven men were searched out and killed. Seven were shot in the yard of the women's section of the prison, and two more were gunned down in the "dog house," a large box under a stairway that had been the home of Captain Davis's bull terrier. Another man, Manuel Politz, was dragged out of the prison and hanged from a lamppost at Treme and St. Ann Streets. Antonio Bagnetto was discovered by Wickliffe hiding under the pile of corpses in the women's yard and was hanged in a tree in front of the prison.

In less than an hour after the execution party had entered the prison, Parkerson announced that the work of the lynch party had been completed.

A few minutes later, they marched out the front prison doors with Parkerson hoisted onto their shoulders like a conquering hero.

While some newspapers denounced the murders, most were pleased by what had occurred. In an interview, Mayor Shakespeare declared, "I do consider that the act was—however deplorable—a necessity and justifiable. The Italians had taken the law into their own hands and we had to do the same." Similar statements were made by other officials, and the general public was happy to see the Mafia's hold over the city broken. A new song, "Hennessey Avenged," made the rounds and became quite popular.

For a short time, the killings threatened international relations. Italy recalled its ambassador and severed diplomatic relations with the United States. The government demanded reparations and punishment against the leaders of the lynch mob. Eventually, the affair was settled when Washington paid $25,000 to the men's relatives in Italy.

The murders did not end the presence of the Mafia in New Orleans, despite what the newspapers of the time wanted their readers to believe. They did leave an impression on the local members, though. Carlo Matranga, who took over leadership of the Mafia in New Orleans until the early 1920s, took a place in the background and issued orders that were carried out by front men. This would remain a tradition through modern times, and rarely would anything illegal be pinned on local crime bosses.

Perhaps the most notorious of these crime bosses was Carlos "Little Man" Marcello. Born in 1910, Marcello came to Louisiana as a baby. His family settled in Algiers, the community across the river from New Orleans, and he started out as a small-time hood. By the 1940s, he had moved into the big business when he went to work for New York gangster Frank Costello in the slot machine racket. In May 1947, he was made head of the local Louisiana crime family and was said to have organized a number of murders, including (if rumors are to be believed) the Kennedy assassination.

At his federal bribery trial thirty-four years later, Marcello swore that he was nothing more than a humble tomato salesman employed by the Pelican Tomato Company—although he did own a little property, which was estimated to be worth $30 to $40 million. His eventual conviction kept him in jail for six years, but in 1989, he returned home to resume his life as a husband, father and grandfather of eleven. Carlos Marcello died in his sleep in 1993 at the age of eighty-three.

THE AXEMAN'S JAZZ

NEW ORLEANS'S MOST MYSTERIOUS UNSOLVED MURDERS

One of the most mysterious, and still unsolved, frenzies to grip the city of New Orleans came in the years of 1918 and 1919 with the arrival of the enigmatic "Axeman." Who was this strange and terrifying creature? Was it a man bent on revenge, a crazed serial killer or perhaps something worse? The period of death and bloodshed that was reigned over by this allegedly supernatural creature is still remembered as one of the darkest times in the city's history. Many believed the "boogeyman" had come to New Orleans.

In May 1918, the Axeman, as he came to be known, arrived in New Orleans. His coming would begin a period of terror that would last for the next year and a half. With the fall of darkness, the residents of New Orleans would spend each night listening to every sound and nervously looking at every shadow. They would open their newspapers with trembling hands each morning. It seemed no one in the city was safe.

To this day, the identity of the Axeman remains a mystery.

On May 23, 1918, an Italian grocer named Joseph Maggio and his wife were butchered while sleeping in their apartment above the couple's grocery store. According to the police, the killer had entered their home just before dawn. He had chiseled out a panel in the rear door of the apartment and slipped inside. He had struck each of the sleeping Maggios once with an axe and then slit their throats with a straight razor. Mrs. Maggio was found on the floor with her head nearly severed from her body. Joseph Maggio was sprawled half out of bed. The razor lay on the floor in a pool of blood, and the axe, as blood-soaked as the razor, was found on the steps going out into the backyard. There was a small safe in the room that was open and empty, yet more than $100 was found beneath Maggio's pillow, and on the dresser was a small pile of Mrs. Maggio's jewelry, including several diamond rings. The police stated that they did not believe that robbery was the motive, although the killer had opened the safe to make it look like it was.

In rooms on the other side of the house lived Joseph's brothers, Andrew and Jacob. They discovered the bodies after hearing moaning and strange sounds coming from the other side of the wall. They went into the other bedroom together and found Joseph half out his bed and still alive. They called the police at once. The police arrested both men after a neighbor reported that he had seen Andrew coming home some time between 2:00 and 3:00 a.m. Later in the morning, detectives made a curious discovery. Written in chalk on the sidewalk, a block away from the house, were these words: "Mrs. Maggio is going to sit up tonight just like Mrs. Toney."

Investigators began digging into old files, looking for possible cases that matched the Maggio murders, and to their surprise discovered that three murders and a number of attacks against Italian grocers had taken place in 1911. The murders bore a striking resemblance to the Maggio crime in that an axe had been used in each and access to each home had been gained through a panel in the rear door. These earlier crimes had been thought to be a vendetta of terror organized by the Mafia. The police and the Italian residents of the French Quarter braced themselves for the worst.

In the meantime, Andrew and Jake Maggio were in jail swearing their innocence. Andrew admitted that he had been out late, celebrating his call to service in the military, and had come home drunk. Both were respectable, hardworking men, and they insisted they had nothing to do with the murders of their brother and sister-in-law. They were released from jail on May 26 and cleared of any suspicion.

The police continued their investigation, and several suspects were questioned and let go because of a lack of evidence. Then, just over a month after the murders of the Maggios, a second crime occurred.

On June 28, a baker named John Zanca made his morning call to deliver bread and cakes to a grocery store owned by Louis Bossumer. The store was closed when he arrived, so he went around back to where Bossumer lived with his common-law wife, Annie Harriet Lowe. The baker did not want to take a chance of the bread being stolen if he left it out in front of the store. When he reached the back door, he stopped and stared in horror—a lower panel on the door had been carefully chiseled out. Zanca tried to open the door, but it was locked. Then, moments later, it burst open, and Louis Bossumer stumbled into the doorway. There was blood streaming from his head. Zanca grabbed the man and eased him back into the house, where he found Annie lying on the bed, bleeding from a ghastly head wound. Both victims were badly injured, each struck with an axe. Zanca immediately called the police and Charity Hospital.

The police believed that Annie had been attacked on the porch that was located on one side of the living quarters, based on the amount of blood that they found there. She had then dragged herself or had been carried to the bed, possibly by Bossumer. An axe that belonged to the grocer was discovered in the bathroom, still dripping with blood.

After she regained consciousness in Charity Hospital, Annie first claimed her attacker had been a stranger. She said that she had awakened in bed with the man standing over her. He was a white man with dark hair that stood almost on end, wearing a white shirt that was open at the neck. Her story changed a short time later, and this time, she was on the porch when she was attacked and Bossumer was the one who attacked her! And, by the way, she told the police, he was a German spy.

During this time of worry about the war, the authorities took Annie's claims seriously. Neighbors gossiped about Bossumer, a Polish immigrant who spoke a number of languages, including German. Could he have tried to kill Annie and then wounded himself, in an imitation of the Axeman, perhaps because the woman knew too much about his activities?

The police were skeptical about how Bossumer could have fractured his own skull with the axe but were ruling nothing out. On August 3, doctors at Charity Hospital performed surgery on Annie. Two days later, she died, but before she did, she stated again that it was Bossumer who had attacked her. He was arrested at once and charged with her murder.

The Axeman chose that night, August 5, to strike again.

Edward Schneider, a young married man, was working late that evening, and it was after midnight when he arrived home. When he reached his bedroom and turned on the light, he was horrified to find his wife unconscious on the bed, her head and face covered with blood. Mrs. Schneider, who was expecting a baby in a few days, was rushed to Charity Hospital. She remembered seeing a tall, phantom-like form standing over her bed and she remembered screaming when the axe fell, but nothing else. She ended up with a large gash in her head and several missing teeth. Luckily, she recovered and gave birth to a baby girl less than a week later.

The police searched the Schneider home, but there were no clues to be found. To add to the general confusion, the Axeman had entered the house through a window instead of through the back door. As usual, though, nothing was stolen.

During the early morning hours of August 10, Pauline Bruno, age eighteen, and her younger sister, Mary, were awakened by strange noises coming from the bedroom where their uncle, Joseph Romano, was sleeping. Pauline crept to her uncle's door and peered into the room. She saw a man standing next to her uncle's bed. She later described the man as "dark, tall, heavy-set, wearing a dark suit and a black slouch hat." Pauline screamed, and the man just seemed to vanish. Joseph Romano lurched out of bed, staggered through a door on the other side of the room and collapsed on the floor in the parlor.

Pauline and Mary ran over and helped Romano into a chair. There were two large cuts on his head that were bleeding profusely. He managed to speak to the girls: "I've been hit. I don't know who did it. Call the Charity Hospital." Moments later, he fainted.

Romano died two days later in the hospital. The police found that all of the Axeman's "signatures" were in place. An axe was found in Romano's backyard, covered in blood. The panel of the rear door had been cut out. Nothing in the house had been taken, although Romano's room looked as though it had been ransacked. The only thing that was odd was Romano was a barber, not a grocer like so many of the earlier victims had been.

By this time, hysteria was sweeping through the city, especially in the Italian neighborhoods. Families divided into watches and stood guard over their relatives as they slept. People went about with loaded shotguns and waited for news of the latest "Axeman sightings." On August 11, the killer was rumored to have been seen in the neighborhood of Tulane and Broad masquerading as a woman. A manhunt was organized, but without success. On August 21, a man was seen leaping a back fence, but despite a quickly organized search party, he escaped. Were these sightings real or merely fright-fueled imaginations at work?

While most of the so-called sightings can be attributed to panic among local residents, the Axeman did leave some tangible evidence behind. On August 11, a man named Al Durand discovered an axe and a chisel lying outside his rear door in the early morning hours. The door had been damaged but had apparently proved too thick for the killer to cut through.

In late August, the rear door of Paul Lobella's combination grocery and residence was chiseled through. No one was home at the time. The same day, another grocer named Joseph Le Bouef reported that an attempt had been made to chisel through his rear door in the night. Awakened by the noise, he had frightened the intruder away. An axe was discovered on his steps. The following day, another axe was found in the yard of A. Recknagle, who was also a grocer. Chisel marks were found on his back door.

On September 15, a grocer named Paul Durel found that someone had attempted to cut through his rear door. A case of tomatoes that had been resting against the inside panel had foiled the attack.

Then, as mysteriously as he had come, the Axeman vanished for the next six months.

During the early morning hours of March 10, 1919, the Axeman struck again. Iorlando Jordano, a grocer in Gretna, just across the river from New Orleans, heard screams coming from the living quarters of another grocer across the street, Charles Cortimiglia. He rushed over and entered the apartment to find Mrs. Cortimiglia on the floor, blood gushing from her head, and the body of her two-year-old daughter, Mary, clutched in her arms. Charles Cortimiglia lay silently on the floor nearby, drenched in blood.

Jordano tried to take Mary from her mother's arms, but she wouldn't let the child go. He got wet towels from the bathroom and tried to bathe her face and that of her husband. Cortimiglia was still alive but fading fast. Frank Jordano, Iorlando's young son, ran over to try to help. His father sent him to call an ambulance. Both of the Cortimiglias were taken to the hospital with fractured skulls. They survived the attack, but Mary was dead.

When the police searched the property, they found all of the familiar signs of the Axeman: the back door panel chiseled out, a bloody axe that belonged to Charles Cortimiglia on the back steps, nothing stolen. It was obvious that the Axeman had returned.

As soon as she was able to talk, Rose Cortimiglia told what she had seen that night. She had awakened to find her husband struggling with a large man in dark clothing who was armed with an axe. As her husband fell to the floor, Mrs. Cortimiglia held Mary in her arms and begged her attacker for mercy, at least for the child. But the axe came down anyway, killing the little girl and fracturing the skull of her mother.

Following the Cortimiglia attacks, New Orleans was again filled with terror. Immediately after the attacks made the newspapers, the police received numerous reports of chiseled door panels, axes being found and dark, heavy-set men lurking in neighborhoods, particularly around grocery stores. Many residents, particularly Italian grocers, appealed for police protection.

Police superintendent Frank Mooney announced that he had assigned a special task force for uncovering the perpetrator the attacks. He expressed the opinion that he was "sure that all the crimes were committed by the same man, probably a bloodthirsty maniac, filled with a passion for human slaughter."

On Friday, March 14, 1919, the editor of the *New Orleans Times-Picayune* received a letter from someone who claimed to be the Axeman. The letter appeared as follows:

Hell, March 13, 1919

Esteemed Mortal:

They have never caught me and they never will. They have never seen me, for I am invisible, even as the ether that surrounds your earth. I am not a human being, but a spirit and a demon from the hottest hell. I am what you Orleanians and your foolish police call the Axeman.

When I see fit, I shall come and claim other victims. I alone know whom they shall be. I shall leave no clue except my bloody axe, besmeared with blood and brains of he whom I have sent below to keep me company.

If you wish you may tell the police to be careful not to rile me. Of course, I am a reasonable spirit. I take no offense at the way they have conducted their investigations in the past. In fact, they have been so utterly stupid as to not only amuse me, but His Satanic Majesty, Francis Josef, etc. But tell them to beware. Let them not try to discover what I am, for it were better that they were never born than to incur the wrath of the Axeman. I don't think there is any need of such a warning, for I feel sure the police will always dodge me, as they have in the past. They are wise and know how to keep away from all harm.

Undoubtedly, you Orleanians think of me as a most horrible murderer, which I am, but I could be much worse if I wanted to. If I wished, I could pay a visit to your city every night. At will I could slay thousands of your best citizens, for I am in close relationship with the Angel of Death.

Now, to be exact, at 12:15 (earthly time) on next Tuesday night, I am going to pass over New Orleans. In my infinite mercy, I am going to make a little proposition to you people. Here it is:

I am very fond of jazz music, and I swear by all the devils in the nether regions that every person shall be spared in whose home a jazz band is in full swing at the time I have just mentioned. If everyone has a jazz band going, well, then, so much the better for you people. One thing is certain and that is that some of your people who do not jazz it on Tuesday night (if there be any) will get the axe.

Well, as I am cold and crave the warmth of my native Tartarus, and it is about time I leave your earthly home, I will cease my discourse. Hoping that thou wilt publish this, that it may go well with thee, I have been, am and will be the worst spirit that ever existed either in fact or realm of fancy.

The Axeman

The people of New Orleans did their best to follow the Axeman's instructions to the letter. Restaurants and clubs all over town were jammed with revelers. Friends and neighbors gathered in their homes to "jazz it up," and midnight found the city alive with activity. Banjos, guitars and mandolins strummed into the night while Joseph Davilla, a well-known local composer, created the theme song for the night. He titled his composition "The Mysterious Axman's Jazz" or "Don't Scare Me Papa," and in typical New Orleans fashion, it became a huge hit. The cover of the sheet music, published by World's Music Publishing Co. of New Orleans, features a drawing of a frightened-looking family playing musical instruments in their living room as a young woman peers nervously out the front door.

When the sun rose the next morning, it was learned that not a single attack had occurred that night. Even though it's doubtful that every home was filled with the sounds of jazz, the Axeman passed the city by, perhaps satisfied by the celebration that was held in his honor.

On August 10, a New Orleans grocer named Steve Boca stumbled from his home on Elysian Fields Avenue with axe wounds in his skull. Dripping blood, he managed to make it to his friend's home about a half block away. The friend, Frank Genusa, treated the wounds as best he could and then called for help. The police who searched Boca's house found the classic signs of the Axeman, including the chiseled door panel and the bloody axe left lying on the floor.

On September 2, a local druggist named William Carson heard a noise at his back door as he was reading late at night. He got his revolver, called out several times and then fired through the door. When he went outside, he saw no one around, but the police officers who rushed to the scene found what they believed were the marks of a chisel on one of the door panels.

Then, on October 21, the Axeman returned for one final slaughter.

Early that morning, Mrs. Mike Pepitone, the wife of a grocer, awoke to hear the sounds of a struggle in the room next to her own, where her

The cover of the sheet music for "The Mysterious Axman's Jazz (Don't Scare Me Papa)," inspired by a gruesome, unsolved string of murders in New Orleans.

husband slept. She reached the door just in time to see a shadowy man disappear through a door on the opposite side of the room. Mike Pepitone lay on his bed, soaked with blood. He had been butchered, and blows had rained down on his head and body, spraying gore onto the walls, ceiling and floor. Mrs. Pepitone and her six children, sleeping just down the hall, were not touched.

When the police arrived, they found the usual signs of the Axeman, including the chiseled door panel and the discarded axe. Mike Pepitone was dead, and his wife could provide no clues about his killer. The case was as hopeless as the others before it.

The police could do nothing more than wait for the monster to strike again. No one knew it then, but the Axeman would not return. His reign of terror was over. The Pepitone killing was the last murder attributed to the Axeman. He was never seen or heard from in New Orleans again. No one would ever learn the true identity of the Axeman—or would they?

More than a year after the Axeman's final appearance, on December 2, 1920, a former New Orleans man named Joseph Mumfre was shot to death in Los Angeles. He was walking down a busy street one afternoon when "a woman in black and heavily veiled" stepped from the doorway of a building, a revolver in hand, and emptied the gun into Mumfre. He fell dead on the sidewalk, and the woman stood over him, still holding the gun, making no effort to escape.

The woman was taken the police station, and at first, she would only say that her name was Esther Albano. She would not reveal the reason why she killed Mumfre. Days later, she changed her mind and confessed that she was Mrs. Mike Pepitone, the widow of the last victim of the New Orleans Axeman. She explained why she shot Mumfre: "He was the Axeman. I saw him running from my husband's room. I believe he killed all of those people."

The New Orleans police were immediately drawn into the case and began working to try to untangle the mystery that might possibly link Mumfre to the Axeman murders. Some curious coincidences were revealed during the investigation. Mumfre had once been the leader of a band of blackmailers in New Orleans who had preyed on Italians. He had also been (for a separate matter) sent to prison just after the first axe murders in 1911. In the summer of 1918, he was paroled at the same time the Axeman appeared again. Immediately after the Pepitone murder, Mumfre left New Orleans for California, and strangely, the Axeman vanished, as well.

Despite these coincidences, there was no real evidence to link Mumfre to the Axeman. Even the newspapers, which would have loved to see a solution to the mystery, pointed out that the dates of Mumfre's release could have been a coincidence. He might have been Mike Pepitone's killer, but the rest of it was all conjecture.

Mrs. Pepitone was tried in a Los Angeles court in April. She entered a guilty plea, and the proceedings were brief. Her attorney claimed that it was justifiable homicide, and while this was disregarded, she did have the sympathy of the court. She was sentenced to ten years in prison but served less than three and subsequently vanished into history.

Were the Axeman murders solved?

Most residents of New Orleans didn't think so, and it remains an unsolved case after all these years. Was Joseph Mumfre the Axeman? Or were there actually several killers, all working together to terrorize the Italian community? Or was the maniac actually what he claimed to be all along— "the worst demon that ever existed either in fact or in the realm of fancy"?

All we can say for sure is that the Axeman did vanish from New Orleans in 1919 and never returned. It is unlikely that we will ever know anything more than that. The Axeman came, haunted the city for a time and then disappeared without a trace, leaving one of the great mysteries of American crime in his wake.

BIBLIOGRAPHY

Arthur, Stanley Clisby. *Old New Orleans*. New Orleans, LA: Harmanson Publishing, 1954.

Asbury, Herbert. *The French Quarter*. New York: Alfred A. Knopf, Inc., 1936.

Davis, William C. *The Pirates Lafitte*. New York: Harcourt, 2005.

Huber, Leonard V. *New Orleans: A Pictorial History*. New York: Bonanza Books, 1980.

Kane, Harnett. *Queen New Orleans: City by the River*. New York: William Morrow & Co., 1949.

Lunde, Paul. *Organized Crime*. New York: DK, 2004.

Lynn, Stuart. *New Orleans*. New York: Bonanza Books, 1949.

Rose, Al. *Storyville New Orleans*. Tuscaloosa: University of Alabama Press, 1974.

Saxon, Lyle. *Fabulous New Orleans*. New Orleans, LA: Robert Crager & Co., 1928.

————. *Old Louisiana*. New York: Century Co., 1929.

Saxon, Lyle, Robert Tallant and Edward Dreyer. *Gumbo Ya-Ya*. Cambridge, MA: Riverside Press, 1945.

Schwartz, David G. *Roll the Bones: The History of Gambling*. New York: Gotham Books, 2006.

Tallant, Robert. *Ready to Hang*. New York: Harper & Brothers, 1952.

Taylor, Troy. *Haunted New Orleans*. Alton, IL: Whitechapel Press, 2000.

ABOUT THE AUTHOR

T roy Taylor is the author of more than seventy books on history, crime, mysteries and the supernatural in America. He was born and raised in Illinois and currently resides in an undisclosed location in Chicago.

Visit us at
www.historypress.net